# THE
# MISERY
# OF
# DREAMS

Chasing a Dream, The Price of Pursuit, and the Lessons
of the Journey

Dr. Tarra Faulk
@iam_drfaulk

This book is dedicated to my husband, my two daughters, and two sons who have showed me compassion, love, and patience despite my shortcomings. Also, thank you to my mother, father, sister, brother, nieces, nephews, extended family, and friends. You all have shaped the person I am and stood by me and supported me through every joy and struggle of my life. Thank you for your unconditional support in allowing me to serve.

Stopping by Woods on a Snowy Evening by Robert Frost

Whose woods these are I think I know.
His house is in the village though;
He will not see me stopping here
To watch his woods fill up with snow.

My little horse must think it queer
To stop without a farmhouse near
Between the woods and frozen lake
The darkest evening of the year.

He gives his harness bells a shake
To ask if there is some mistake.
The only other sound's the sweep
Of easy wind and downy flake.

The woods are lovely, dark and deep.
But I have promises to keep,
And miles to go before I sleep,
And miles to go before I sleep.

May this poem, my favorite, inspire you to stop and consume the
beauty of your surroundings but then press on the journey you
were divinely purposed to make.

# TABLE OF CONTENTS

# INTRODUCTION

## What is your dream?

My dream was to become a doctor. I have wanted to be one ever since I could remember, so I set a goal to achieve it. I went to college. I went to medical school. And finally, I became a doctor!

It was a long-term, inspirational vision that I created for my future. It was my way of securing a solid future for myself that would ensure my independence, my freedom from Sacramento, and my contribution to society by helping the sick get well.

Dreams represent an individual's highest aspirations, desires, and ambitions and can be related to various aspects of life, including career, personal growth, relationships, health, and more. It is, by very definition, an almost unattainable imagination, a vision beyond expectation. But it also represents our most envisioned being. The best we hope to achieve. Now, once you have completed your dreams, and because you have 100 percent ownership of your dream intellectual property, it should result in endless joy and happiness. Right?

I envisioned going to college and being so talented and sought after that I would enter rooms, and people would say, "look at her," "She is amazing," "Let's give her scholarships and acceptances into the best medical schools, etc., etc." Well, none of that happened; the road was much longer than I anticipated, and once I completed all the steps to become a doctor, my feelings didn't measure up; in fact, they were the opposite of joy; they were more like pain and despair.

I knew that pursuing my dreams would require determination and focus and often involve taking risks and facing challenges, but I had hoped for a sense of fulfillment, purpose, and a life well-lived on the other side. I did not anticipate what it might feel like to be living in my dream career. Perhaps I imagined ear-to-ear smiles when I woke up, butterflies, and birds chirping sing-alongs, like in Cinderella, and ending the day with a smile and an overwhelming feeling of accomplishment at the day's success. While these feelings weren't completely absent from my existence, beginning two years after completing my fellowship training, I realized that my positive feelings about my profession and my dream job, which took so long to come to fruition, were rapidly dwindling.

I knew there would be days or weeks of hard work and the resultant fatigue. I knew that life as a physician would be challenging or even hard. But this hard? Simply put, I was unprepared for what it would feel like to be an ambitious working mother and wife, and all the accompanying stuff smacked me in the face. Hard!

As I neared the time to decide to launch after completing my fellowship and my commitment to the military, I didn't feel empowered; I felt stuck. I felt like my life at that time was not what I thought it would be, and initially, I could not figure out why. I thought it might be because I made the wrong decision in my career. I thought I wasn't strong enough to deal with all the extra stuff that went into being a doctor, or my support system and friends weren't good enough. I re-evaluated everything: my relationships, mental health, and diet. I contemplated changing everything in my life. These feelings had nothing to do with the day-to-day patient care required to be a doctor. Everything else needed managing or required my attention; the things that are the threads of you as an individual who also happens to be a doctor. All I know for sure is that I felt disillusioned and didn't quite know why. It wasn't just one thing but a multitude of things. This period of intense self-reflection forced me to study myself, and now I want to teach you what I learned. Your pain will lead to your passion, leading you to your purpose.

Do you remember the phrase, "be careful what you wish for"? I now know that the quote has nothing to do with the work it takes to achieve something, but instead, it speaks to the sacrifice and the grit required to keep it. Your dream may differ from the rosy picture or lifestyle you envisioned, and you may feel disappointed. You may ask yourself, "What did I get myself into?" or "What was I thinking?" And those questions will lead you to wonder if these are normal thoughts or feelings. Is it normal to feel like you worked so hard to achieve something but no longer feel excited about it? So soon after you completed it? I had all these thoughts and more, so I started putting together this book during those moments of desperation as I contended with my decision even to become a physician.

Here are some truths. The struggle is actually real. And even when you achieve your dreams, challenges will exist. Another reality is that not everyone will cheer for you while you pursue your dreams and goals. Just because you've earned a degree and attained one of the highest roles you could envision in medicine, you'll sometimes feel out of place, disrespected, or misunderstood. Your family and friends will challenge you by contradicting your medical knowledge and recommendations and questioning your decisions. There will be life events that derail your timelines, and other random things will happen to and around you that you were not expecting. While any of these things, circumstances, or challenges alone may not completely derail you, together, they can cause you to feel so defeated that you may want to abandon everything.

## Is this normal?

Imagine that shortly after you have spent four years in college, six years in a career but still working toward your dream, four more years in school, another three years in training, and another two more years in training on top of that. You finally are working in your dream job, but you feel miserable. Worse, those last 19 years had some pretty crappy moments you had to drag yourself through. Worse still is the realization that anything else you decide to do now would require you to change course completely. What would you do? Would you feel comfortable talking to someone about it? That was my story, and despite a pseudo-real consideration of jumping two ships, I didn't. Instead, I altered my course and continued transforming it into what it is today. I have clarity about my path forward and know that one day, I will have my dream job and feel good in it and my dream life with my dream schedule AND, so can you.

No matter who you are and what profession you are in, I want to tell you these feelings ARE normal, and many people experience these same feelings, and most are too afraid to say them aloud. I encourage you that the struggle is merely part of the victory. You cannot have the rainbow, so to speak, without the rain, and you cannot have a beautiful forest of trees without the pain and many years of growth.

I have exceeded my largest dreams and gone on to do more than I had ever imagined. Finally, I am in a place where I have overcome the negativity of my feelings and have matured to a position where I can collect the tools necessary to succeed in my career and concurrently in my life. But getting here was less pretty and glamorous of a path than I thought it would be. For me, life hasn't been a crystal stair (homage to Langston Hughes). It's been hard. It's been a struggle. During it all, I thought I would finish medical school and residency and then go on to work in my clinic or at a hospital that I loved and that I would do that for the rest of my career.

I wrote this book to normalize talking explicitly about the struggle it takes to succeed at hard things. The overused cliché phrase "the struggle is real" does nothing to prepare you for or even commiserate the battles you will face or are facing. It is normal to work hard every day toward beautiful goals and then lose yourself. I want you to know that despite your doubts and fears and the challenges you face, living a goal-driven life is admirable, and having big dreams is the best way you can affect the trajectory of your life. I know that your ambitions are inspired by the generations behind you, cheered on by those who surround you, and linked to the generations ahead of you. And so we need to talk about how blind ambition can destroy you. We fool ourselves into thinking we were meant to live stressed, tired, and overwhelmed—the "no pain, no gain" mentality. I experienced much pain while becoming a doctor. And while I felt isolated at once, I now know that my experience was not unique to me. If we all shared similar experiences, there have to be more of us who then second-guessed our decision to go into medicine altogether.

But just like physical training, there is healthy pain that makes you sharper and unhealthy pain that is meant to indicate injury. You need to hear my story and learn why and how I changed my career trajectory with all its nontraditional packaging. Finally, I want to share with you the tools I have gained along the way so that you may fill your toolbox and meet the demands of your life to prevent or at least be ready for any future feelings of despair. And just like Cinderella sang, "No matter how your heart is grieving, if you keep on believing, the dream that you wish will come true".

Your struggle will be real, but you will be stronger than any struggle you face!

# GLOSSARY OF TERMS AND CONCEPTS

I didn't write this book exclusively for people in the medical field. In fact, my target audience is any disillusioned young professional who isn't happy with their current work or standing in their profession and is thinking about making a significant change. More specifically, those professionals who want to drive, not be driven by the corporate machine, and build a path for themselves in their profession.

Here is a list of terms and concepts specific to medicine that I didn't want you to shift your attention to look up.

## Path to becoming a Physician

To become a physician in the United States, an individual must complete a bachelor's degree, typically (but not required) in a science-related field, followed by four years of medical school. After graduation, physicians must complete a residency program, typically lasting 3-7 years, to gain practical experience and specialized training in a particular area of medicine. Some physicians may also choose to complete a fellowship for further specialization. After completing residency or fellowship, physicians must pass licensing exams and obtain a medical license to practice in their state. Physicians must also complete continuing education and maintenance of licensure requirements throughout their careers to ensure ongoing competency in the field.

## Rotation

A medical rotation is a period of specialized training where medical students or residents work in a particular medical specialty or department for a set period, typically 4-12 weeks. They gain practical experience and knowledge under the supervision of experienced physicians. Rotations begin in medical school and continue in some manner throughout medical training.

## Intern (medical)

A medical intern is a qualified medical graduate undergoing supervised training in a clinical setting to acquire the practical skills and knowledge required for medical practice. Their duties include observing patient care, performing physical examinations, and assisting in medical procedures. On the other hand, a summer intern in a business is a temporary employee who typically has limited experience in the industry and is hired to assist with day-to-day tasks, such as data entry, research, or administrative tasks. The roles are vastly different regarding responsibilities, required qualifications, and the nature of the work performed.

## Resident

A medical resident is a physician who has completed medical school and is undergoing further specialized training in a hospital setting. Historically, residents lived in the hospital (a resident of the hospital) to be readily available for after-hour emergencies and to gain more practical experience. This practice began in the late 1800s/early 1900s. Today, residents typically have set work hours and aim to maintain a work-life balance, though many still have little free time outside the hospital during training. The competitive residency program prepares physicians to provide high-quality patient care while advancing their knowledge in their chosen field of medicine.

Fun fact: I lived in the hospital during one of our month-long medical school rotations. I did that rotation twice.

## Fellow

A medical fellow is a physician who has completed a residency and is pursuing additional training in a specialized area of medicine. Fellows work alongside attending physicians to gain expertise in their chosen field, conduct research, and develop advanced clinical skills. Fellowships typically last 1-3 years.

## House staff

"House staff" refers to medical residents, also known as resident physicians. These are licensed doctors who are in the process of receiving advanced training in a specific medical specialty.

House staff typically work in hospitals under the supervision of attending physicians. They provide direct patient care, make medical decisions, and learn about the diagnosis and treatment of various medical conditions. The term comes from the historical practice of housing resident physicians near the hospital where they worked. While this is no longer a common practice, the term continues to refer to this group of medical professionals.

## Attending vs. Staff Physician

There is a difference between staff physicians and attending physicians. Staff physicians are employed by a healthcare organization, such as a hospital or clinic, and are responsible for providing medical care to patients. They may work as part of a team or independently and supervise other healthcare professionals, such as residents and fellows. On the other hand, attending physicians are typically senior-level physicians who oversee the care provided by staff physicians, residents, and other healthcare professionals. They may also provide direct patient care and are responsible for making critical medical decisions, such as determining the appropriate course of treatment or making the final diagnosis.

In some healthcare organizations, the terms "staff physician" and "attending physician" may be used interchangeably. However, generally attending physicians have a higher level of responsibility and more advanced qualifications than staff physicians.

## Physician vs. Doctor

The terms "physician" and "doctor" are often used interchangeably to refer to someone qualified to practice medicine. However, there are some subtle differences between the two. A physician is a medical professional who has completed medical school, obtained a medical degree (such as an MD or DO), and is licensed to practice medicine. The term "physician" is often used in a more formal or academic context and can refer to doctors specializing in different areas of medicine, such as psychiatrists, pediatricians, or cardiologists. "Doctor" is a more general term that can refer to anyone who has obtained a doctoral degree in any field, not just medicine. However, in common usage, "doctor" refers to medical doctors.

# Nephrologist

A nephrologist is a medical doctor specializing in diagnosing and treating kidney-related diseases and disorders. Nephrologists manage a wide range of kidney conditions, including chronic kidney disease, kidney stones, electrolyte disorders, hypertension, and acute kidney injury. Nephrologists are also trained in the management of patients who require dialysis or kidney transplantation. Nephrologists typically complete a 3-year internal medicine residency followed by a 2-3 year nephrology fellowship. They work closely with other healthcare professionals, including nurses, dietitians, and social workers, to provide comprehensive care to patients with kidney-related disorders.

# Chief Medical Officer

A Chief Medical Officer (CMO) is a high-ranking executive in a healthcare organization responsible for overseeing the organization's medical policies, procedures, and practices. The CMO provides medical leadership, expertise, and guidance to the organization's management team and physicians, ensuring that clinical care is safe, effective, and high-quality. The CMO also plays a key role in developing and implementing clinical programs and initiatives and ensuring compliance with regulatory requirements. The CMO may also represent the organization to external stakeholders, such as government agencies, professional organizations, and the media. In the Air Force the CMO is called the Chief of Medical Staff or SGH.

## CHAPTER ONE

# DREAM

"Nobody wants to show you the hours and hours of becoming. They'd rather show you the highlight of what they've become." – Angela Duckworth

Christopher George Latore Wallace, also known as Notorious B.I.G. or simply Biggie, was an American rapper from Brooklyn, New York, who, at the age of 24, was shot multiple times in a targeted drive-by shooting and died due to his injuries. If you were to Google search his name, a lot would come up about his personal life: growing up poor, being an aspiring rapper, a love triangle that included a wife and two girlfriends, his involvement in the feud between East Coast and West Coast rappers and the fact or fiction about his participation in the robbery of Tupac Shakur, a west coast rapper.

On Wallace's first and only album released while he was alive, a song called Juicy begins, "It was all a dream, I used to read Word Up! Magazine, Salt-N-Pepper, and Heavy-D up in a limousine. Hanging pictures on my wall, every Saturday Rap Attack Mr. Magic Marley Marl" The song is a narrative recount of his aspirations of becoming a rapper intertwined in his rags-to-riches story and a transitional account of his rise to fame in the entertainment and rap industry. This prose is akin to a physician reminiscing when they were just an aspiring doctor watching medical sitcoms like E.R. or Scrubs or reading published journal articles while envisioning themselves a successful doctor and then speaking of their success once they made it.

As an 11th grader, I was tasked with picking my career, interviewing someone in that field, and writing an essay about it. Without prompting or hesitation, I decided to become a neurosurgeon. I found a neurosurgeon in the phone book and completed my assignment. I don't recall much of the conversation except that I was a bit nervous to reach out initially and that he was kind and answered all my questions. We likely exchanged pleasantries, and he probably offered himself for a follow-up phone call. I, however, never spoke to him again.

Before this fateful assignment, when I was about 10 or 11 years old, I thought I wanted to be a model or a singer. Neither of these panned out, mainly because I was too short, per the modeling agency, and I was too shy to sing in front of peers, let alone on a national stage.

After I realized these would not be fruitful career paths for me, I don't recall much about career goals until that assignment in high school. However, I remember a program called Project Pipeline, where I, along with other students across the districts in Sacramento, were bused from our local campus to the University of California at Davis on Saturday mornings to participate in the Science, Technology, Engineering, and Mathematics curriculum. While all my friends were sleeping in on Saturday morning, I woke up super early for a half-day of education.

While I did not enjoy having my Saturday mornings robbed, subconsciously, the experience planted a seed. I believe that seed to be the only link between my decision to go into a career devoted to science and life-long learning because I cannot pinpoint any other trigger in my life that would make me want to go into medicine. And so, in 11th grade, I declared that I wanted to become a neurosurgeon; I began planning and set out on that dream journey.

That dream journey was, let's say, interesting. I had no point of reference, no internet to search from, and no one in my family to guide me through the process. My sister was a college graduate, but she was off serving in the Army, and I knew nothing about her academic career. The point here is that I decided on some lofty, unimaginable dream without any roadmap to get there. That did not deter me, though; I drew out a timeline that included completion of high school, four years of college, four years of medical school, and then specialized training in surgery. I at least had the understanding that my desire to become a neurosurgeon could change, as evidenced by my initial timeline ending with medical school- perhaps this was something that the neurosurgeon mentioned when we spoke. Still, college and medical school were a constant in the plan. One day, while at Barnes & Noble, adjacent to the Arden Mall, I found a brain anatomy coloring book that my dad happily bought for me, and I carried that book around for about a year-looking nerdy as hell in front of all my friends and cousins.

The song Juicy, by Chris Wallace, AKA Notorious B.I.G., was released in August of 1994, so let's say it served as part of an inspirational soundtrack as I progressed toward my newfound dream of becoming a surgeon. I went to college with a plan: four years of college followed by four years of medical school, and then five or more years in surgery residency and subspecialty training—no gaps, no relationship goals, just school and the expectation that it would be hard work.

I completed college on an Air Force scholarship, and I did well academically but not well enough to gain the Air Force's blessing to defer and attend medical school. Okay, what do I do now? I rewrote the plan: complete college, followed by four years in the Air Force, then four years in medical school, and then five or more years in surgery and subspecialty training. I had options, so I chose what I thought would be a brief but exciting career in military intelligence and proceeded to train and work through that process while still planning to return to my medical school timeline.

Four years later, after marrying my husband, my first commitment to the Air Force was coming to an end. I was thriving at work, winning significant awards and accolades, and successfully leading projects. Some said I was on the general's path, which meant I was progressing and hitting milestones that could lead me to become a general officer one day. I loved what I was doing then and had met so many wonderful people, but something was missing in my life: the void of an unattained dream.

I wanted to become a doctor and did not feel that my job in the military provided the fulfillment and job satisfaction I thought was inherent to the study and practice of medicine. What should I do? I separated from the military without any solid plan, except that I would be working toward one goal: getting myself into medical school.

Five months before my separation from the Air Force, a huge television show called Grey's Anatomy began its world domination of Thursday nights. Grey's Anatomy's original release date was March 27th, 2005, but I couldn't watch it. I was paralyzed by it. I wasn't in medical school like or when I had planned. My grades were good, but I was having difficulty with admission, and my Medical College Admission Test (MCAT) scores weren't adding up to greatness, perhaps partly because my second test preparation was interrupted by a military deployment. It made me sad-mad that even fictional characters could play physicians better than I was able to become one in real life, and I just couldn't watch it.

I believe in dreams. I encourage the setting of goals to achieve big dreams. In fact, I created Dream Lab Podcast, where we provide interviews, stories, and tips for goal-setters and go-getters to be inspired to live a life of purpose. In the referenced verse from Wallace's song Juicy, he talks about his dream of becoming a rapper, how he used to follow rappers' careers, and fantasized about being a rapper while flipping through the pages of rap magazines. At the time, he had the benefit of rapping about his dream, successfully having entered the rap ranks as a famous rapper and his success at that moment. If we compare Christopher Wallace's climb to musical genius to an average person's goal-setting and rise to professional success, we will see many similarities. What you probably don't know and won't easily find in your Google search is that Christopher learned diction and phrasing from a jazz saxophonist when he was a teenager in Brooklyn. This jazz artist would give him homework that included scatting and listening to the music of Ella Fitzgerald and Charlie Parker.

He also practiced vocally with speed and agility exercises. Wallace's sound was unique, and when people speak of his rapping ability, they hone in on the clarity and enunciation of his words, his rhythm and unique flow, and his ability to tell a story that the listener could easily follow in his music. His stardom was about ten years in the making, but he had a dream of becoming a rapper and could see the fruits of that labor.

I spent the remainder of 2005 taking the MCAT, revising my personal statement, and applying to medical schools. I also prepared for failure once again by applying to intelligence jobs because, at that point, I doubted my abilities to achieve these dreams. I was second-guessing myself and the trajectory of my life. I was questioning if I had made up this magical story of becoming a doctor, and maybe it wasn't happening because it wasn't supposed to happen. The uncertainty of my future raised many doubts, like, am I really meant to be a physician? Am I pushing this along, but it wasn't in God's plan- hence the reason why everything isn't lining up for me? What other than medicine could I possibly do at this point that would bring me joy?

Finally, though, I received interviews at a handful of medical schools, was accepted at two and ultimately chose the Georgia Campus, Philadelphia College of Osteopathic Medicine. School began in August 2006 and on September 21st, 2006, I watched my first episode of Grey's Anatomy at a watch party, surrounded by my medical school classmates.

# NOTES

CHAPTER TWO

# MISERY

"Misery: (noun) a state or feeling of great distress or discomfort of mind or body - Oxford Languages

Medical school was little of what I had imagined and much of what I hadn't. It was like "Mean Girls", an experience I never had during high school, plus a mix of immaturity that I did not know was possible in people in their twenties. It did not help that our school was only in its second year of existence as a branch campus of one of the oldest medical schools but was masquerading as if their parent campus wasn't linked. As a result, there were weird faculty decisions, "interesting" curriculum and grading policies, and unnecessary work and stress for us as students.

After two years in medical school, I was sleep deprived, lacked an emotional outlet other than my husband, and even he couldn't really grasp the magnitude of what I was going through. My friends stopped inviting me on trips and to events like weddings and birthdays, and even if I was asked, solo leisure travel didn't make sense with all the sacrifices being made for me to attend medical school.

I lost interest in and time for any hobbies I once enjoyed, like dancing, crafting, and photography. We also lacked a church home. I had a small group of friends in medical school, and they kept me grounded. We were a friend group that morphed into a study group and a family bond. At that time, we traversed the most challenging stage in our lives together. I was busy studying and Roderick with work and commuting, but when I look back on that time, I chuckle because we had no children and few extra responsibilities. We said we were busy, but we didn't really understand the triviality of using the word busy back then. Now, we are truly busy. Back then, we were just faux busy.

I gave birth to our first daughter one week before graduating from medical school. She was the most beautiful and precious thing I had ever encountered. I was praised for "choosing" the right time to have a baby, a common question physicians-in-training ask. When is the best time to start a family? Indeed there is no "best time," but unbeknownst to me, this was a very peculiar time to have an infant child. We remained in Georgia for six weeks following my delivery, and then we were off to Texas to start my intern year.

My husband, my true-life partner, and I worked hard to raise our daughter during the most stressful time in my life. Or, maybe I should say, the first most stressful time in our lives. I started one month behind my peers but jumped right in on the in-hospital (inpatient) service. It was a busy service. I missed all the pre-start social events and therefore had no friends. I was also unique because I was the only female intern with a child.

I had made the decision that I wanted to nurse for a year. Because this was before any mandates that required dedicated rooms for nursing mothers, I was pumping in random corners of the hospital or my car if I had the time or was traveling between hospitals. I even pumped while driving, which I do not recommend because it added to my baseline fatigue, which could be considered an impairment. With all the tubes and equipment, it was a distraction and potentially a hazardous situation. I also needed to pump during our practice exams and standardized testing at testing centers. That required me to make arrangements in advance to pump in the bathroom, my car, or an available room which most of the time was a storage closet or a stranger's office.

Pumping demanded a lot of my time. From going to find a place, setting up and pumping, then cleaning, drying, packing up, and trying to find a safe place to store the milk, all while answering repeat pages from nurses, physicians, and other hospital staff. To save time, I would grab lunch and attempt to pump while eating, but that backfired a little because pumping made me lose my appetite. Inevitably I would either get busted in on while in one of the resident rooms that had no locks, paged to put in some order, or summoned to the bedside of a patient for some random thing that probably could have waited for any one of the twelve or more patients that I was managing on the service. I was stressed. I was kicking my little duck feet as fast as I could beneath the surface but barely remaining afloat.

At that time, we also had something called a thirty-hour call. Call on those days went something like this: you arrived early in the morning to prepare for rounds.

Rounds are when the medical team visits all the patients on their team as a group to review the patient's status and develop a care plan. Official rounds are with the attending physician, and teaching would occur throughout. Team individuals do pre-rounding and chart reviews to obtain the information needed for rounds. The time before official rounds are used to catch up on what occurred since you last saw the patient or checked the chart. Also, you could start on order writing, note writing, and the planning needed for the day if there was extra time. Rounding also allows you to speak with nurses, review laboratory and radiological study results, and speak to consultants and other specialists about the patient.

At some point during a 30-hour day, and hopefully, once you had your existing patients squared away, your team would go "on call" and begin evaluating and admitting new patients. Call would go on into the night, and we would then remain in the hospital overnight to track the progress, develop and execute plans for these newly admitted patients, and follow up on the preexisting patients. Our team would also cover the patients followed by other teams, i.e., cross cover, overnight while our colleagues went home to rest. We would also write the new patient's admission documents and orders. We were expected to get some sleep at night, but usually, that was interrupted by the needs of the patients. In the morning, we rounded on our old and new patients and prepared to brief our attendings and residents on all the patients we were managing.

We remained in the hospital for about 6 hours more the day after we reported and were free to go. Having completed all the rounding, patient discussions, writing of orders, and checking up on patients, I would drive home exhausted, falling asleep at stops and veering out of the lines while trying not to kill myself or anyone else on the way. Dog tired, the question would be whether you stay, take a nap or risk it all, and drive home immediately. Most of us chose the latter to get the freak out of dodge as fast as we could to be with our family or before anyone would attempt to work us some more.

I wasn't going home, though. I would drive to my daughter's daycare and nurse her. I missed her and wanted to bond with her. The daycare staff prepared a rocking chair for me to sit on and nurse. They somewhat understood that I wasn't there to take her with me because I hadn't slept well in over a day but was simply there to nurse her, snuggle her, and then return her to them so I could rest at home alone. Then I would drive home, shower, and crash until it was time to prepare dinner. Theoretically, one good thing about the 30-hour call was that you didn't have to report back until about 18 hours after the call ended, allowing for a sustained rest period, albeit after 30 hours of work.

In my first year, I received a few mediocre ratings, but one was exceptionally ruthless, stating I was the worst intern he, the attending, had ever seen in my written review. He said none of this during our face-to-face evaluation, and I attribute that to his cowardly avoidance of confrontation. My co-intern on that service, whom I thought was a rockstar, received a similar but less harsh rating from that attending, and he printed off his evaluation and kept it in his back pocket. From that experience, though, I internalized a valuable lesson, first, to make my expectations in the teaching and clinical setting known, and second, as an attending, I make my expectations known. I provide feedback to my students, residents, and fellows early and offer ways/tools for their improvement if they perform below what I think or what the standard describes as acceptable.

During my first year, I developed a deep seeded scorn. I had no colleagues in a similar situation- married with a child. I spent all my free time pumping and rushing home, so I could not forge solid relationships. I was lonely by circumstance, and I felt like it was just too hard to do everything, and it weighed on me. My colleagues couldn't be sympathetic to my situation because most

23

had no idea what was happening to me. I did not want to draw attention to my personal life or seem as if I were complaining. I was trying to make it through, no more and no less.

Nurses at that time were my worst enemy. At my primary hospital, they were vicious, passive-aggressive monsters. The spectrum ranged from blatantly ignoring me to demanding my time. I could stand at the nurse's station begging for acknowledgment, get the door slammed in my face during shift change, or have orders barked at me: "Sign this order." "Come to the bedside now" "You're doing that wrong." "This person needs a diet order." "This person needs this; this person needs that."

Everyone had free reign to show their disdain for us trainees vocally- from the cleaning contractors to the white coat exchange personnel. I knew people who would machine wash their white coats before exchanging them to avoid being chastised by one particular white coat police officer who would accost you for not bringing your white coat back at the earliest sign of dirt.

I began eating lunch in the break room on the 4th floor because it was where I spent most of my time. Because of this, I thought it would be a great primary place to store my pumped milk as well. That would make 2 freezers since I also had one down on the 1st floor where I had clinic.

After eating my lunch there a few times, it became obvious that this was not a shared break room for all employees but a nurse's break room. I was an outsider. I did not immediately catch on though. The ringleader would occasionally make indirect comments about my storing breast milk in the freezer. Never anything overtly rude, but I could tell she was hinting at something. Apparently, she disapproved because one day, my milk was bagged and moved to a different location in the freezer and inside the travel cooler without needing it to be moved. Another nurse later told me who had moved the milk.

I was angry but disappointed at the time because this was another woman. Why didn't she understand? Feel empathetic? Because she was a crappy human. That was my thinking at the time. Just add her to the list of people not on my side. She was not rooting for my success.

Like many others, I had no refuge, and this wasn't something you talked about openly; you just came to work, tried your best, went home, and then tried to be better the next day.

But I did complain about how I hated everything to my husband, and one day he got fed up with my whiney complaints. His response changed everything. He told me that he and Gabby were making great sacrifices for me to be able to train to become a doctor. I wasn't at home with them most of the time; he was the primary caregiver, homemaker and worked. Because of my schedule, we didn't get to do as much as we wanted. So, if I hated everything I was doing, I needed to either stop so that we all could end our suffering or drive on and try to make the best out of my situation. His words woke me up inside and forced me to dig myself out of my rut. It worked.

When I transitioned from being an intern in my first year of training to becoming a resident, it opened the door to a few freedoms. It added additional challenges like carrying the infamous Medical Officer on Duty pager. You were no longer a scared intern but more of an angry barrier. For some reason, as a resident, you take on the hospital's guardian role and vow to let no unnecessary patient breach the walls of your fort. That manifested as a constant, vicious battle with anyone who attempted to admit a patient who could be managed elsewhere. Infamously, that frequently involved the battle of Medicine vs. the Emergency Department. My hospital had a particularly cunning yet conniving set of emergency physicians, and they seemed to want to admit everything that passed through their doors. They refused to back down, and we refused entry. These rifts had nothing to do with patient care; they were more a war of ego and might. I took these battles personally. They were the enemy. Being at work on call days was stressful primarily because of these types of emotionally consuming war of words. The Emergency Department wasn't the only challenger— Medicine vs. Critical Care, Medicine vs. Cardiology, Medicine vs. Surgery, and on and on.

I had my son during my second year of residency. I was a better mom and physician but still learning in both roles. The talk with my husband made me realize that I didn't just want to survive this experience; I wanted to thrive. I wanted to be the best physician. I wanted to be so good that I wasn't just reacting to disease; I wanted to have the knowledge to predict illness and make diagnoses early to give my patients their best shot at health and recovery. I also needed to learn to be a working mother actively. I also needed to work at that while giving myself grace and avoiding ruminating about mom guilt.

After a year of spending all of my free time somewhere pumping, I could finally be seen and recognized as part of the team, and as such, I began to make peer connections. Some senior residents had children, and a few women attendings offered their support. I became an even better doctor, navigating motherhood and residency more easily in my third year but still harboring feelings of anger exacerbated by sleep deprivation and loneliness. I was planning to apply to a fellowship program because I was tired of being treated like crap in general internal medicine, and oh! Nephrology sounded fascinating.

# NOTES

## CHAPTER THREE

# REGRET

"Worry empties today of its strength" - Corrie Ten Boom

TO WHOM IT MAY CONCERN:
RE: Tarra Faulk

I am a Vascular Surgeon in Atlanta and have had the opportunity to host Tarra Faulk for a one month Vascular Surgery rotation. The purpose of this letter is to offer my strong support in her application for residency in General Surgery. During our month together, I found Tarra to be engaging, extremely disciplined, and mature well beyond what I would consider the norm. I strongly feel she is well suited to pursue a career in surgery. She has an outstanding fund of knowledge and has exhibited an even higher level of commitment to learning. In fact, she spent hours drawing each of the major vascular families in the body with precise detail completely independent of any recommendations from myself. I have never seen this before in a medical student and I simply use this to illustrate her dedication an interest in learning.

In summary, she has the maturity, drive, and knowledge required to exceed in a general surgery program and I feel she will become a very strong resident and asset to her institution. If there are any questions or comments, I would be pleased to discuss Tarra anytime on the telephone.

Best regards,

This letter, written on my behalf, was one of the three letters of recommendation submitted for my application to the Air Force general surgery residency program. I had decided against neurosurgery during medical school after meeting the neurosurgeon who taught our neurology block. Not only did his work not sound exciting, and our study of the neurological pathways did not hold my interest, but he, as a person, seemed "different," and I could not see myself in him or his work.

I then decided that vascular or cardiothoracic surgery appealed to me, and I scheduled both rotations. The vascular surgery rotation was in Georgia, close to home, and the cardiothoracic surgery rotation was in Los Angeles, California. Before both specialty surgical rotations, I completed a general surgery rotation at Travis Air Force Base.

My first general surgery rotation was amazing. We arrived at the hospital early to round, ate breakfast, and then went into the operating room. I loved scrubbing in, donning fresh scrubs, and walking over to the assigned operating room. I would then go to the large stainless steel surgical scrub sink and grab one of the soap-impregnated sponge and nail pick packs, break it open, and then use the timer to scrub my hands clean. Next, I would enter the operating room, receive assistance with dressing, and wait for the attending to arrive. I especially loved when the nurses asked about my glove size before my arrival, a simple gesture that meant they cared about me and my experience. I loved the feel of being first assist, seeing inside the human body, the smell of cauterized tissue through a surgical mask, and even the smell of my hands when the case was finished and we had taken off all our protective gear. But my favorite thing was being allowed to close and show off my suture skills.

My vascular surgery rotation turned out to be an intimate look into my future as a Nephrologist. As a medical student on this vascular surgery rotation, I was first assist on many arteriovenous fistula creation cases, which are the lifelines for hemodialysis patients. It is a surgery where a vein in the arm is attached to an artery to allow for hemodialysis (manipulation of the blood by a machine to keep a person alive who has kidney failure) to be performed. This is a very delicate surgery that requires magnification eyewear, a headlight, tiny scalpels and needles and thread, heparin injected into the vein with a blunt metal needle tip, and a lot of patience.

Next, I journeyed to Los Angeles for my last surgery rotation of medical school after securing the most interesting living arrangement I had ever experienced. There weren't official housing arrangements for out-of-state rotators, but people housed rotating students by letting them stay in their homes. One particular person's home was occupied by the time I reached out, but the owner of that house had a neighbor who had never housed students but was interested in helping students while earning some extra money. I spoke with this man by phone and email a couple of times, and we settled on a payment amount of $844 (the same as the other students paid) for the month and I was on my way. He was a divorced screenwriter with a couple of kids.

When I arrived, I met a nice quirky man, his ex-wife, their daughter, their son, their daughter's friends—it was her birthday, their dog and cat. I learned that since our connection and my arrival, he had been called for a job out of state and would no longer be at the house during my stay that month. He asked if I wouldn't mind caring for his pets while he was away.

The house was humongous, atop a hill with a gorgeous view, but the beauty of that view was never fully realized as I spent dusk to dawn at the hospital on weekdays; a blazing fire made the air murky, and the time I did spend in the house, I was partially terrified because being alone in a new environment scared me a bit.

I had a room with a private bathroom, and I quickly learned that it was likely the cat's favorite hangout because right before I went to bed that first night, I felt something land between my feet and curl itself up for bed. One night when I returned home, the cat bolted out the door and did not return after I opened the door several times to look for him. He did not return the following day, and I began to worry. Finally, that night, when I called the owner's ex-wife to explain the situation, she reassured me that this was normal behavior and that the cat would eventually return. Whew- a sigh of relief. The cat did eventually return, but I cannot remember how long it took for it to do so. I would let the dog out in the mornings and take it out for walks in the evening.

Exploring Los Angeles as an adult, hanging out with new and old friends, and leisurely living when I wasn't in the hospital were great experiences, but the actual surgery rotation was awful. It was the cardiothoracic surgery service, and our attending specialized in esophagogastrectomies, a surgery where the entire esophagus (the tube that essentially connects the mouth to the stomach) and part of the stomach are removed, usually after a cancer diagnosis.

This all-day surgery was fascinatingly grueling, one I had never experienced before. The surgery would begin early in the morning after our morning rounds and breakfast. The patient would start in the prone position (lying face down). The surgeon would spend the morning entering the chest cavity through the back and freeing up the esophagus, which normally sits inside the chest but behind such structures as the lungs and the tube that goes from the nose to the lungs.

The first part of the surgery would last until lunchtime, and then once completed, the physician-led team would leave the operating room to have lunch and rest. During that time, the nurses and technicians would remain with the patient to prepare for the next part of the surgery, which involved flipping the patient to the supine position (lying on their back) and prepping the front side of the body for surgery. Once ready, we would come back and proceed to enter the chest through the front and complete the removal of the esophagus and part of the stomach, and then reconstruct the now missing structure using the stomach and/or part of the colon.

During one of these surgeries, when I was first assist to the program director, in an attempt to anticipate his move, I reached into the surgical field with my shears to cut a suture. The shear met with an object that turned out to be the surgeon's hand, and he jerked his hand back, cursed, flailed his arms, stepped away from the surgical field, and then a nurse removed his top glove from one hand.

He continued to curse and began yelling at me about my mistake and the importance of his hands. Meanwhile, I stood there, frozen, on my step stool, my left hand holding the tip of the shears while my right hand held the shears to my chest. When he returned to the field, he said something to me, and then we continued the case without any teaching or comment other than orders and instructions. I have since judged that to have been an exaggerated theatrical performance because he was double-gloved and did not remove the second glove, and he did not go missing after the case to participate in any mandated post-needle stick or exposure activities; nonetheless, lesson learned.

The program director and his father, the former program director and at the time an active surgeon in the hospital as well, were infamously known at what was, if not the most, one of the most malignant surgery training programs in the country. Rumor has it that the father would spend a typical day with the surgery team, rounding early in the morning and then preparing for and completing his surgical cases. Once his surgeries and charting were complete, he would go home, eat dinner with his family, shower, and do whatever else he deemed necessary. At the same time, the students, residents, and fellows remained in the hospital because he required a second formal rounding time in the evening to follow up on his patients and the team had to wait for his return to discuss the plans and then complete any additional charting or order entry that resulted from the last rounds. Only after that was the team released to go home. This may seem like a far-fetched story, but this was exactly how his son, the program director and my rotation attending, ran the service. We would be in the hospital until 8 PM or later because we had to wait for his return and this was every day while he was our attending.

During this rotation, two people came to the forefront of my mind. I recalled a female general surgical resident from the Travis Air Force Base surgery rotation. I remember her on the phone with her apartment manager because she was late on rent. I assume there was no direct deposit way for her to pay at that time, the problem not being that she couldn't afford her rent but that she was in the hospital for so long daily that she could not get the check to the office during their business hours.

The next surgeon in training was at the program in Los Angeles. She was overweight and out of shape and spent all her time in the hospital. I only mention the overweight and out-of-shape part not to shame her but because she said it constantly. She was in her fourth or fifth year in surgery training, and her time still wasn't her own, not even for physical health. Though I sensed a love for surgery that was only suppressed by the circumstances of training, I also deduced that she was not very happy with her personal life. Even though she wanted to date, it wasn't easy due to her chosen specialty.

These two women began to play louder and louder in my head during this rotation. I was already married, but we started talking about kids and the future. I didn't see myself in these women, and the inherent stress of training seemed not to be limited to the training environment in the trainees of the profession; it was also present in the lives of the attendings. I could see myself in the operating room but nowhere else.

These events and the replayed mental ruminations were enough to make me completely switch course and try to remove my application, already submitted, for the general surgery residency program. I had minimal time to decide about my future, and I felt in my gut that the right thing to do was something else. But what?

There was one other rotation that I really enjoyed and that was Endocrinology. So, I called up the physician with whom I rotated, described my problem, and then asked him for a letter of recommendation.

I was unable, however, to retract my application but instead was able to add Internal Medicine as my primary specialty while keeping General Surgery as a secondary. Both programs accepted me, but I entered Internal Medicine as a Categorical Intern because of my new ranking.

My decision to change from Surgery to Internal Medicine was pivotal in my life. It was a time, probably the first time, I made a decision not based solely on my individual goals and aspirations, but I took into account my husband and the children we had not yet brought into the world. I was no longer an individual making decisions who happened to be married. But I was a wife, considering our future and how that might look in one specialty versus another.

Now and then, I feel a tug in my heart and a fullness in my throat when I walk past the operating room or see a surgery team on rounds in the hospital, and I wonder how life would have been different for me if I were a surgeon. Would I still be married? Would I have as many children? Would I be happy and fulfilled?

You may be experiencing doubts, regrets, or questioning some decisions from your past. Just know that regret is merely a human emotion that arises when we feel disappointed, sad, or remorseful about a past decision or action. This feeling that you made a decisional mistake or the sadness you feel because you think you missed out on an opportunity you idealized a life around is a form of natural grief. But just because you created imagery about what life should be for you doesn't mean it was for you. You can gain insight into your values and priorities by reflecting on your past experiences, and the knowledge gained can help chart a course for your future. While I will never know the answers to those "what if" questions, I know now that my change in direction put me on the right path.

Now, I am so happy to be a practicing Nephrologist. My journey into medicine began with the dream of becoming a surgeon, and nothing I experienced or learned was regrettable. Nothing occurs by accident. This reckoning with the reality of my decision was often painful, but it helped me grow. It led me to become more self-aware, and only now am I better equipped to recognize and take action when it is time to make difficult decisions about my family and future.

Regret is simply a type of worry that has no purpose. Instead, let us self-reflect, correct, and then move forward.

# NOTES

CHAPTER FOUR

# DESPAIR

"We watch the house officers work endlessly during their nights on call, we listen as they wish their patients would die so that they could get a few hours more of sleep...And by the end of our training, not only do we no longer still have the desire to help our fellow man, we don't even want to be bothered by them. "- Robert Marion, M.D.

There are some things you tolerate because you know they are time limited. Medical training has a very interesting way of teaching resilience one month at a time while dangling in front of you the prize carrot that tricks you into continuing the game year after year. You tell yourself, "This will be over in a month." Then it's "I can survive anything for a month." But then, every month, there is an escalation of challenges, abuse, and trauma. Then you become conditioned, and things keep worsening, but you are numb to your surroundings because you have morphed into a toxic, hardened beast. But you trudge on because this tiny voice tells you it will all be better soon. And so, you dig in and push yourself even harder; patiently waiting for that glorious day when you elevate to the position of Staff Physician.

Going straight into fellowship, I took unresolved feelings of inadequacy, triumph, trauma, resilience, embarrassment, hurt, and defeat but pressed on. As a Nephrology Fellow, I felt abused by our staff, other hospital staff, and the other house staff at the three hospitals we managed. Nephrology Fellows could be called at any time, day or night, and each call involved a sick patient who required our attention. Most frustrating were the consults on very ill patients with poor prognoses because it almost seemed as if we were the gatekeepers to heaven. It was as if a sign on the door read "No Entry Without a Nephrology Consult." This forced us into intimate end-of-life conversations where others refused even if we didn't know the patients well. We were also called for guidance when other services feared calling their fellows or attendings for help.

We were multi-hatted, often serving as the senior medicine residents, the critical care fellows, and the senior surgery residents. We directed others to give blood, find their bleeding source, and all sorts of other logical recommendations that were missed by the person calling. We were called to dialyze people who skipped their regular treatments. We slept in our cars while waiting for dialysis nurses to arrive so we could see our patients on dialysis. We were the backbone of the hospital and, as such, we were sleep-deprived and angry but learning from the best and feeling good about our work.

Once, I was on a two-person team responsible for the kidney care of forty patients, which was insane for two people. We were in the hospital until well after 8 PM while triaging new consults and working through our task lists for the patients we were following. Despite our long days and all the time spent in the hospital, we as fellows could anchor on one simple fact, this will only last one month, and we can endure anything for a month, and it will all get better when we become Attendings.

Psalm 30, verse 5 says, "Weeping may endure for the night, but joy cometh in the morning," and our "morning" would be the eventual graduation from all our medical training.

Through it all, as my amazing husband held everything together at home while attending law school and caring for our two children, those last two years of training were the best educational experiences ever.

The aftermath, though, was painfully tactile. I was raw. I graduated from fellowship, and the dust began to settle. I passed my nephrology board examination and was starting my practice in the Air Force, and that's when reality set in. I initially thought I wanted to be an Air Force Nephrologist, eventually working my way to clinical expert and continuing my practice in the civilian sector. However, life once again threw me for a loop.

After years of rigorous training, I arrived at my desired hospital as an independent physician, ready to embark on a career I had long aspired to. However, the reality of the job turned out to be quite different than I had anticipated, and this realization shook me to my core. While I had some inkling of this halfway through my fellowship training, I was too invested in what I had already started, so I soldiered on.

During my rounds with the hospital nephrology team, we found ourselves discussing the challenges of our day-to-day lives, and my co-fellow jokingly, but perhaps also somewhat seriously, suggested pursuing another career entirely. Though it was a fleeting thought, it underscored the absurdity of the situation we found ourselves in; having invested so much time, money, and energy into this field, it seemed like there was no other course but to see it through to the end.

This conversation happened before I encountered patients who were challenging, outside of the medicine, to manage, such as the one who loudly berated me for not prescribing him opiates or, the one who falsely reported pain during dialysis to show me his backside. It also occurred after enduring the bullying and belittling that are all too common in physician training. However, it was a turning point for me, as it marked the beginning of my questioning whether I had made the right choice in my career.

Over time, I faced more emotionally draining situations, such as being called into the hospital in the middle of the night to attend to patients who missed their life-sustaining treatment (hemodialysis) or guiding unsupervised physicians who were afraid and uncertain. However, despite the nuances of patient care, these were not at the heart of my frustration and despair. Chronic fatigue ruins your spirit. It puts you on edge. It makes you respond to everything in anger. It robs you of compassion and replaces it with bold arrogance. I had become just that over nine years of medical training. Five of those years, spending countless hours in the hospital learning to diagnose, treat, and care for others while not necessarily receiving that same level of care for myself.

Once I finally finished, I was making my schedule while prescribing medications and treatment plans that did not require the approval of another physician; I hoped to feel accomplished and overwhelmed with joy and satisfaction. I had made it through the toughest part of my career, and I expected validation with joy and peace. I did not expect demanding patients who did not want to participate as a member in their healthcare team. I did not expect to work so closely near the edge of my scope of practice due to staffing shortages. I did not expect to have a dialysis unit without a social worker and have to fight to get one part-time. I did not anticipate the barriers to providing quality patient care. I naively thought I would come to work, be a doctor, do doctor stuff, and then go home and start over the next day. I looked around at the mounting roles and responsibilities required to do just the doctor part at my institution, in my organization as a whole, and felt it was too much. I needed an out. I began to ask myself, what have I gotten myself into? Why am I here? Is it too late to become a nurse? At least they have a union.

# NOTES

CHAPTER FIVE

# COMEDOWN

"I don't want to come back down from this cloud. It's taken me all this, all this time." - Bush

In September 2018, three years after completing my fellowship in Nephrology, we lived in California, about 45 minutes from where I grew up. We had three children. In those three years, I worked my way up from Staff Nephrologist to Medical Director to Nephrology Element Leader, which is a military way of saying Nephrology Division Chief.

I was a full-time clinician, taking care of patients while overseeing our clinic's business operations, including a small hemodialysis outpatient unit, outpatient clinic, and inpatient operations. I enjoyed all my work, and gradually, the funk of training began to purge from my body.

I was in a good space. I had begun distance running for pleasure after work, providing a cathartic mental a physical release I never knew existed. My family was close by, and trips to visit were frequent. My sister's commute from work allowed her to drop in for dinner often. The kids were in good schools, enjoying their friends, and we also had a network of great friends. We joined an amazing church and thrived spiritually by leading a small group.

Professionally, I was struggling to decide my next steps. The year 2019 would mark the end of my military commitment, and I was preparing myself to apply for civilian and Veterans Affairs (VA) Nephrology and/or leadership positions. I knew I needed more leadership experience to transition into a civilian leadership job, but I also felt nervous about full-time nephrology practice in a civilian medical group. Being a civilian nephrologist is different than being a military nephrologist because you usually have to cover multiple hospitals, similar to what we did during fellowship training, but also manage a higher number of dialysis patients to be a contributing member of a practice and earn adequate pay.

Additionally, I knew that I would be starting from the bottom of the ranks if I were to join a civilian practice because I would be the team's newest member. It wouldn't matter that I had practiced elsewhere or had prior experience as a leader; I would be the latest hire, working long hours trying to grow my patient numbers and taking unfavorable shifts, again because I was the newbie.

The thoughts in my mind weren't because I thought I was incapable. Still, the contemplation was whether I wanted to start again from the bottom and the fact that leaving would also be a decision to defer my opportunity for retirement from the military.

In real terms, I was taking stock. I was thinking about my life and career, what I wanted to accomplish professionally, my rank and the opportunities accessible to me at the time or the near future, my husband's career, and our children's options. I went into medicine because I wanted to help people, but there are many ways outside of the practice of medicine that contribute to healthcare delivery. I saw injustices and things that required change during medical education and training. For example, diversity, equity, and inclusion in education, medical school learning models that were based on archaic foundations, work hour restrictions for trainees, parental leave during training and as staff, pumping rooms for employees, clinic staffing models, need for longer patient appointments in primary care, a shift from volume-based compensation to anything else. These were things that, if improved, would improve the lives of physicians and, therefore, their care delivery.

We as a profession had made significant gains in some of these areas during my transition from training to a young physician leader, but there was and still is much more work to be done. There are tables void of physician leaders where decisions that impact our lives are being made, and I felt the need to be at those tables. During this time of reflection, it was becoming apparent that my most significant potential for influence was not just in the patient care setting but in the leadership arena as it pertained to leading physicians and advocating for their wellbeing while creating a space for patient care that was not only safe but made sense.

Additionally, at the time, I held the rank of Major and was set to promote to Lieutenant Colonel in 2019 if I remained in the military. If I stayed at that particular hospital and was promoted, I would continue to work clinically while taking on leadership roles as an additional duty without an opportunity to advance until I became a Colonel five or so years later. Also, as part of my clinical time, I was required to serve as the attending on the Internal Medicine Rotation for the Family Medicine Residency

Program. Many problems with that setup and execution put specialty care providers, like me, at risk. I knew it was time for me to go.

In September 2018, I wrote the following journal entries:

- shake the dust; the dust is a distraction to your destiny

- dust is an offense [something that offends]; you don't have a strategy for offense [for how to respond to being offended]
- because that thing that was meant to destroy you did not

- what is the most painful thing in your life? Nurture the pain in your life. We have to climb out of pain.

- And while I was contemplating this book, I wrote the following:

- Merriam-Webster defines misery as suffering and want resulting from poverty or affliction (a cause of persistent pain or distress; great suffering). Affliction or self-inflicted pain. I am in pain, constantly dealing with a gnawing pain of mental anguish and distress. A self-inflicted pain of sorts. But one I cannot escape. Because an escape might equate to a greater weakness, weakness far greater than physical strength but a lack of mental endurance, perseverance, resilience. The mind is very powerful.

I began to rehash all the negative things I experienced during medical school, residency, and fellowship, finally feeling my suppressed emotions for the first time. I believe that was where the words stemmed from in my journal entries. I had experienced a mental onslaught of pain and suffering from training and everything else around me. Still, when those things were happening, I could never process them or work through and heal from them; they were like open wounds manifesting as misery at a time when I should have felt accomplished...satisfied.

At that moment, I learned about something called Arrival Fallacy. A common cognitive bias that can lead people to chase after achievements and possessions in the belief that they will bring lasting happiness and fulfillment. Stated differently, it is the belief that achieving a particular goal or acquiring a specific possession will bring eternal joy and satisfaction. The fallacy can lead people to focus on term goals and ignore the importance of developing positive habits and mindsets which can be sustained over time.

Scientifically speaking, the expectation of a goal's future success triggers the brain's reward centers to produce a feeling associated with pleasure. When you achieve that goal, you have become so accustomed to that pleasurable feeling that when you achieve success, it is less satisfying. As a result, if you don't feel terrific at the completion of your goal, you instead feel disappointed. Others have called this "post-achievement depression," or my favorite description from Melody Wilding in the Forbes article "Why Reaching Your Goals Can Surprisingly Make You Less Happy where she describes it as "a psychological thought trap high-achievers are all too familiar with."

It was like what I imagine coming down from a drug high might feel like. Most likely because I had no new goal to focus on. I was essentially all dreamed out.

So how do you address or treat the arrival fallacy? The most interesting "cure" I found was immediately setting another goal, but there is toxicity in that approach because you aren't really addressing the problem. If goal-seeking were akin to drug addiction, you would jump from one addiction to another. A better solution I discovered included focusing on the "why" and framing life in a manner that would lead to a sustained appreciation of the value of life's work. However, the acceptance of this model must come with the realization that there is no win or culminating event. It will be an endless game where the purpose is to keep "playing the game," not conquer it.

# NOTES

CHAPTER SIX

# PURPOSE

"You have a masterpiece inside you, you know. One unlike any that has ever been created or ever will be. If you go to your grave without painting your masterpiece, it will not get painted. No one else can paint it. Only you." - Gordon Mackenzie

I needed to decide if I would stay in the military or leave, what we call "separate" from the military, which means a personal decision to leave the military before becoming retirement eligible. If I decided to separate, I would then exit in 2019, having served nine years in the military. If that was the plan, I needed to make connections and explore what the nephrology scene looked like in the area so I could easily transition to a group after separation. I probably would not have had much trouble as a physician, but something in my spirit wasn't quite right, and that was the part that made me linger on the decision. At the time, I was having a good run; most of my education was paid for in some way by the military; I had worked with great people, had phenomenal work and life experience, and could not complain. We already talked about the close proximity to my family, which I loved, but we were also close to Napa, San Francisco, Sacramento, and Lake Tahoe. Man! We were eating and drinking well, and our kids were thriving. I must tell you, it was glorious to get a frequent whiff of honeysuckle and hibiscus in the air and have mostly beautiful weather year-round, except for the wildfires.

I felt good about the work I was doing in the lives of my patients and their nuclear circles. I also felt good about the nurturing and mentoring of the junior Nephrologists and staff members in my division. As a Nephrologist with dialysis patients in particular, I formed unique bonds with them, their families, and caregivers.

You see dialysis patients one to four times per month and more times if your patient has complications or other things going on with them that need to be addressed. Dialysis patients are frequently hospitalized, so you also have the opportunity to care for them when they are admitted. That is also where you interact with their family members the most. You become intimately involved in their lives, and they, in turn, treat you like family. Even though I took pride in caring for my patients, I needed more reach. I had more to give, but I was limited in what I could do while caring for my patients daily. I was allowed the opportunity to do both patient care while exploring leadership positions but the burden of doing both wasn't sustainable.

At about the same time, I had decided to be more intentional in my involvement at church, including serving in church, getting my finances in order, and tithing regularly. My pastor at The Father's House in Vacaville, California (Dave Patterson) and a woman whose teachings I was introduced to by that church (Havilah Cunnington) got me on a path I spent the next two years in. I began digging into God's word and what the Bible says about purpose. I prayed and fasted and joined a small group. Next, we led a small group, and I served on a team at church. I wanted to get closer to God, be in a relationship with Him, and intimately know Him so I could distinguish His voice from that of the world. I leaned in, and He responded.

The following are my journal notes from a sermon on great expectations:

- from the book of Romans 4:17-21 and Romans 15:13...expect God for more, let God do the speaking because He can speak things into existence

- learn the source of the promise

- I was listening to hear what He had to say about my situation and learning from what the word had already declared. And also, learning to wait...Romans 4:20

## Romans 4:17-21 (NIV)

[17]As it is written: "I have made you a father of many nations." He is our father in the sight of God, in whom he believed—the God who gives life to the dead and calls into being things that were not. [18]Against all hope, Abraham in hope believed and so became the father of many nations, just as it had been said to him, "So shall your offspring be." [19]Without weakening in his faith, he faced the fact that his body was as good as dead—since he was about a hundred years old—and that Sarah's womb was also dead. [20]Yet he did not waver through unbelief regarding the promise of God, but was strengthened in his faith and gave glory to God, [21]being fully persuaded that God had power to do what he had promised.

## Romans 15:13 (NIV)

[13]May the God of hope fill you with all joy and peace as you trust in him, so that you may overflow with hope by the power of the Holy Spirit.

There were successive teachings on purpose and service.

I felt that God was leading me to the broader service of others in my career. It would require more than the education and experience that I already had, and it wasn't something I could readily do if I separated from the Air Force. These revelations and family discussions led me to remain in the military and apply for a leadership role that would take me away from California.

There are benefits to being spiritually aligned, and as a note to you, my new bestie, I contemplated whether I should include my faith and speak about God and the Bible in this book. I realize that not all my readers will be Christians, and I do not want to unintentionally offend anyone. I am a believer first, and everything else comes somewhere after that. The Bible is a book, a historical accounting of the past, and for believers, so much more. For nonbelievers, the Bible's words, thoughts, and teachings can be considered just like any other book you read. But for believers, the gospel has power and much more meaning. And so when I reference text from the Bible and lessons learned from my pastors and religious leaders, I am hoping that if you are a believer in another religion, an omnist, atheist, or agnostic, you will be able to consider the words in context without any overly religious connotation as I am sure you will find healing and maybe even salvation in these words. I will leave it up to you to determine your definition of what that means to you.

So, by 2018, having redefined and rededicated myself to a purpose, I decided to write a book about my experience. I had a colleague at the time who hated his current position, not the job but everything surrounding his position at the hospital where we worked. He had to make a tough decision to move to another military base in another state just before his final year before retirement because it was his only option to regain his love of medicine and, in some regard, his sanity. He did this in exchange for time because the move meant he would have to extend his time. Despite that increase in time, he felt he could not bear another year at our hospital, even if it meant retiring later than planned. He was enduring many hours in a short-staffed clinic, daily microaggressions because of his race, and lack of top cover support from leadership, and he also internalized and carried the burdens of other providers in our facility. He is an amazing human and skilled physician who had been at our hospital for several years. Still, he could not materialize the changes required to improve the working environment.

There is an essential nugget in that story, which I tell everyone I mentor who is considering leaving the organization because of toxicity. Do not be afraid to move from a toxic work environment. Toxicity within organizations isn't always universal and can be person or location specific. It can be toxic organizational culture or leadership culture, which I can't conceptualize because what I know about culture and the frequency of corporate leadership transitions contradicts the premise of leadership toxicity. If the determinants of culture are predicated by toxic leadership, why then wouldn't the culture improve with the high turnover of leaders?

When toxic organizational culture remains despite leader turnover, it is ingrained in the staff with permanence. My theory is that those without executive power somehow retain the control that drives the culture. In nearly 20 years in the military, I had not seen a person successfully change a toxic culture except when it was a new leadership-driven change. I have witnessed upheavals in leadership, investigations into workplace toxicity against organizations and individuals, the firing of individuals, and even the inability to prosecute offenders because of loopholes; toxicity is hard to change, but the key to success is first identifying it and reporting it through official pathways. As such, while I do not advocate for cowering, I also do not endorse sticking around and enduring toxicity to the detriment of your well-being.

Some people have a way of creating a ceiling for you or making it very hard for you to live in your purpose, and so, unless your purpose in life is to be a heroic vigilante who fights for the rights of good people in the workplace, which is an admirable endeavor…then I suggest you do like my colleague and I did and take your chance at a better situation by moving to another location, job, or organization entirely. You have to decide what is best for you.

# NOTES

## CHAPTER SEVEN

# MISGUIDED

"Not every piece of advice is meant to be taken. You must have the discernment to know which advice is right for you." - Unknown

A dvice is a tool that can be helpful or harmful depending on the advisor's intent and the advisee's use.

Are you familiar with Marie Kondo? She is a professional tidying expert whose brand surrounds helping people organize their homes and transform their lives through tidying by category. Her method includes completely disorganizing, reorganizing by category, and discarding items that do not spark joy. I came upon her book through the recommendation of a friend, and I read half of it before proceeding to go to town in my closet because that is where her hierarchical method started.

I took all my clothes out of my closet, modeled them, paired them with other items in my closet, and touched them to see if they brought on a sensation of joy, indifference, or pain. I got rid of a lot of things and then reorganized my closet. I kept a few items that didn't necessarily spark joy, but I couldn't tell what I felt when I touched them, so I kept them because I couldn't commit to a feeling. I then went on to books and maybe a few paper items.

Then, instead of reading the entire book, I moved on to my parent's home and enlisted all my family members to help. My parents were soon to move into their new home, and I thought it would be a good idea to help them declutter while they were on vacation. They had a lot of things they had accumulated over their lifetime, some old, some nonfunctional.

Unbeknownst to me, there is a tiny part in Kondo's book where she explicitly instructs that this activity is personal and not meant for you to impart to others. But as I said before, I hadn't got to that part, you know, because…80-20.

On the personal front, I never completed the task. I skimmed through the rest of the book and decided it wasn't for me. Later, I found myself looking for clothing items and missing the ones I had ousted to no-joy land. I did not realize that my clothes were my sentimental items which, per the KonMari method, were to be reserved for last.

In the KonMari activity, I undertook a task counter to my lifestyle because I felt the pressure to minimize, but I live in the mindset of overabundance and preparedness. I like preparation to the point of self-containment, which has proven beneficial. An example of this was during the pandemic, while everyone was scrambling for toilet paper, soap, and cleaning supplies, our family did not worry because we had everything. I also like to have ensembles on hand for the various types of events that I might attend. From a cocktail party one night to a family movie screening another, a fundraising event, a speaking engagement, or a business lead lunch or meetup. I like to be ready for anything.

Being super tidy also is very difficult when you have multiple little humans with playful agendas living under your roof. I couldn't commit to the "golden rule" of becoming tidy. Kondo, too, learned this lesson as she revealed she's 'kind of given up' on being so neat after becoming a wife and mother. I wanted to be more orderly, just not the most orderly. In that situation, I didn't have the discernment for that advice to know that the "tidy movement" wasn't a good fit for me.

Advice can provide valuable insights and perspectives, but it's essential to consider the source and context and where you are in your journey. Once guidance is received, one must internalize it, use their judgment, and decide what to do based on their unique circumstances and values. In that sense, advice can be akin to a medical consultation. You take what applies or fits your treatment plan and leave the rest.

Leadership is conceptually very similar to the advising concept. Leadership is just advice from a position of authority. You may disagree with me and counter by saying that it is frowned upon not to do what your boss says, and that may be true if you are working the fries at Mcdonald's but trust me, many midlevel and corporate employees are doing their own thing every day and getting paid top dollar for it. Conceptually, there are more complexities than I am describing here, but there are many similarities.

On the topic of leadership, I have a growing list of authors and speakers recommended to me by my friends and colleagues. The list includes book titles, podcasts, YouTube videos, and blog posts by John Maxwell, John P. Kotter, Stephen R. Covey, Sheryl Sandberg, Brené Brown, and others. But when you dive deep into the conceptual framework of leadership, you will learn that there is no one-size-fits-all leadership style.

Individuals who speak on leadership have been categorized by the leadership genre that matches their speaking topics. For example, I was recently introduced to Brené Brown by an amazing friend. Brené's work primarily focuses on vulnerability, shame, empathy, and building resilience. She is not typically associated with a specific leadership style; however, her insights on organizational culture are similar to the servant leadership style. She emphasizes creating a safe and inclusive environment, building trust and meaningful connections with others, and empowering team members to reach their full potential. Brown's books, such as "Dare to Lead" and "Braving the Wilderness," provide valuable insights into leadership and how leaders can cultivate more inclusive, empathetic, and courageous work environments.

Globally, I don't want to discredit the complexity of leadership and the fact that situations dictate the type of leader required. Nor the understanding that while people tend to lead from one style primarily, it is possible to be fluid between the styles. But, while leadership growth might include an exploration of the other leadership types and the incorporation of different styles, an autocratic leader who successfully makes decisions without the input of others would probably be best served with recommendations that align with "The Art of War" by Sun Tzu, not "Servant Leadership" by Robert K. Greenleaf.

The goal here was to dig deeper into the concept of good and bad advice and good and bad leadership. A common misconception is that everything that sounds good is meant to be incorporated into your life. Another misconception is that for people to advise you, they must look like you or have experiences that mirror yours. To be successful, you must be able to absorb the valuable nuggets from your surroundings. Your boss is a micromanager; okay, learn how to successfully get ahead of them and keep that as a tool should you encounter another micromanaging boss. Your romantic relationship was a failure; okay, what did that person reveal about you and how you could be a better partner in the future? Learn from it and grow in all your relationships.

It is always nice to learn from someone who looks like you or have a model person in your life who has the same values as you do but know that it is not a requirement for you to be successful. Take me for example; It would be hard to find many black, Christian women, physicians, in the military, married with four kids, who also run a nonprofit organization and have a C/D personality. Equally, I would be foolish to think that anyone that did not fit that description could not positively affect my trajectory. I would instead connect with multiple people and discern good from bad and then make it applicable to the situations in my life, making every moment a teachable moment, whether good or bad.

Advice, mentorship, and coaching come in many forms, and every bit of information you receive that advances your status is a win. Equally, great information can be gained from negative experiences. I had had many negative situations where I would force myself to find the lesson, whether that be a trait I needed to unlearn before it became a habit or arming myself with a set of solutions should that event happen again.

As for KonMari and me, I have revisited some principles, like organizing items by category for the entire house, especially with household items and kid toys. The timing of the advice makes all the difference- sometimes you may receive a good word, and you need to put it in your back pocket for a later time.

# NOTES

## CHAPTER EIGHT

# PREPARED

"The goal isn't to live forever; the goal is to create something that will." - Chuck Palahniuk

Have you ever heard the quote, "Stay ready so you don't have to get ready"? I have listened to it so many times, said by so many people, that I would have never guessed it originated with Wesley Snipes as the character Blade. I love this quote; the movie Blade, not so much.

It means that you should stay prepared so that you will be ready to jump on any opportunity when a situation arises.

I am usually an over-packer. When we go just about anywhere, leave it to me to have an umbrella, water bottles for everyone, wipes and extra clothes in case someone has an accident, disposable toilet seat covers- you name it, I have brought it. Also, every day that I go to work, it's the same, my personal laptop because I have professional meetings on Zoom, notebooks, food to last the day, water, a pillbox, an umbrella, extra pens, etc. I always want to be ready just in case something happens because I don't want to be in a situation with panic, disorder, or lost time.

In the professional setting, how does this translate? The answer is more complex.

Grit: The Power of Passion and Perseverance is a book by psychologist Angela Duckworth. She draws on her own research and the work of other psychologists, educators, and business leaders to explain how "grit" can be developed and cultivated. Grit, as she describes, has contributions from talent but is a phenomenon resulting from sustained effort toward a goal or goals that ultimately lead you to success.

This concept can be best described using the following equations from the chapter in Grit called Effort Counts Twice:

Talent x effort = skill
Skill x effort = achievement

Expanding on some of the concepts in her book, Duckworth explains that "Enthusiasm is common. Endurance is rare."

In an example from the book, she talks about her college friend, an international journalist for the New York Times, who won the 2012 Pulitzer Prize for International Reporting for his coverage of the conflict in East Africa- Jeffrey Gettleman. While reflecting on how passion played out in his life, Duckworth explained that his story did not begin with his wanting to become a journalist. It started with a feeling from a place he wanted to return to. On a trip to East Africa in his youth, he connected with the spirit of Africa, and he wanted to make that a part of his life. In response, he built his life around returning to that place, that feeling. He began taking courses in Swahili, returned to East Africa and experienced the same wonder, explored photography, and eventually focused on journalism because it could create a path for him to return to Africa.

Next, he created a deliberate plan based on what he knew about the journalism industry, which included several steps (sound familiar?).

He described it in this way:

"It was a really winding road that took me to all kinds of places. And it was difficult, and discouraging, and demoralizing, and scary, and all the rest. But, eventually, I got here. I got exactly where I wanted to be."

When successful people achieve their dreams, which ultimately should be linked to their passions, the familiar metaphor of passion as fireworks doesn't make sense. As you recall, I falsely associated the two early in my career. As Duckworth explained, fireworks erupt in a blaze of glory but quickly fizzle, leaving wisps of smoke and a memory of what was once spectacular.

But as Jeff's story and my story and so many other stories tell us, passion isn't fleeting. It can be best described as a compass- a guide to something that "takes time to build, tinker with, and finally get right." It may take you on a long and winding road to where you ultimately were destined to be.

Another quote frequently recited is, "To whom much is given, much is required." It originated from Luke, chapter 12, verse 48 in the Holy Bible.

Much is required when you lead a purpose-driven life. And when you expect to flourish in your life, grit, discipline, and preparation will be your best character traits for success.

I am a member of a speaker's bureau, and recently on one of our calls, the topic of how to get more speaking engagements came up. The person who asked the question wanted to speak "as often as possible" monthly. The group leaders respectfully challenged that statement because that was an unmeasurable and unrealistic goal.

If you wanted to become a paid speaker, you wouldn't sit at home wishing for someone to invite you to speak. Instead, you might create a talk on a passionate topic and deliver that talk for free where you think people might benefit from the message. You would hire a photographer to capture you giving that talk. Not only would you have photos of you speaking, but you would also be able to practice and perfect your delivery. You would then create an advertising campaign surrounding your talk that incorporated your talk highlights and the photos you had banked from your free talks. But the process would continue because you would create a new talk every year and repeat the process. Your grit toward your goal of becoming a speaker and your discipline in taking the necessary steps to prepare for the call from a CEO looking for a speaker.

Readiness is the cornerstone of seizing opportunities. From Wesley Snipes' famous quote to Angela Duckworth's exploration of grit, we understand that being prepared extends far beyond physical objects—it encompasses personal growth and professional aspirations. The winding road of passion and perseverance leads us to our desired destinations, where discipline and grit fuel our journey. As we navigate this path, we must internalize some truths (1) significant responsibilities accompany great gifts, and (2) the things we hope to achieve in life will never make their mark if we never get started. With unwavering determination and diligent preparation, we embark on a quest to fulfill our dreams, recognizing that preparedness paves the way to a future beaming with possibilities.

# NOTES

CHAPTER NINE

# EVERYTHING

"And there's a million things I haven't done. But just you wait, just you wait..." - Lin-Manuel Miranda

When I first contemplated becoming an author and the concept of this book in particular, I hadn't completely figured my life out. I didn't know how the story would end or whether that would be outside the military or within it. I didn't yet have that triumphant success story. I knew I was going in the right direction, but I wanted to know if there would be a success story on the other side. As such, I babysat the idea and continued to randomly journal but had yet to commit.

When I finally did commit to completing this book, I knew there had to be at least one person, like me, who struggled to find happiness in something they worked so hard for. It wasn't widely discussed because of the stigma associated with the shame of feeling like you failed at something. And so, I felt this book could help people work through their issues and whatever guilt or shame they harbored during the process.

That stigma evaporated somewhat during COVID when we heard stories about highly educated and experienced professionals exiting from the medical and other fields. During that time, you saw people giving up their careers in exchange for moral integrity, schedule and location flexibility, and just plain freedom from the corporate machine. I was on the career exodus sidelines, cheering for those bold and financially stable enough to do it. They seemed to be taking control of their lives and showing for once that their work didn't define them. It was the freedom to leave circumstances that did not fit their ideal work environment that made me most envious. I could relate to that desire but could never leave my job for so many reasons.

So now, I am writing a book. I am a physician with a growing family and contemplating a considerable change in my profession; I was also expecting a promotion and the responsibilities associated with an increase in rank. Then I made a commitment to myself to write a book.

I have been known to pursue many things at once. One of my toxic traits is that I genuinely believe I can do all things. I like to keep myself busy with the "leave nothing on the table" mentality. And especially if I can get someone else to pay for the opportunity, that is a win-win.

I have two opposing examples of how this has played out in my life.

In the military, there is something called professional military education which is the equivalent of executive organizational education in the civilian sector. Our curriculum is mostly about military history, war strategy, and leadership topics. It does not directly apply to the practice of medicine, but it is the underpinning of military culture.

Take, as an example, my response to an assignment regarding the United States Military Response to the 2010 Haiti Earthquake. What roles can personal relationships play in forming a joint task force? What are some potential benefits or pitfalls of relying, even partially, on personal relationships to achieve goals? My response focused on the importance of strategic messaging and communications in humanitarian assistance and disaster-response missions to allow for the adaptability necessary for teams to respond quickly. I then spoke about personal relationships, strategic agility, intelligence, and cultural acuity. At the surface level, this and the other exercises within professional military education would not help me diagnose and treat autoimmune nephropathy in one of my patients, but the benefit is further reaching. You gain a global understanding of dealing with difficult situations and interacting with and leading people, which are necessary proficiencies.

Professional education becomes more critical as you progress in rank because it shows you are dedicated to the military and your service. Still, it is also a show of commitment and the discipline required to complete a task. Physicians usually opt out of this additional coursework because the risk to their career outweighs the benefits if they desire to remain clinically competent.

I began one course called Air Command and Staff College (ACSC), but it was too challenging to complete because I needed more free time to do it. Eventually, I ran out of time to get it done ahead of my promotion cycle, so I decided not to complete it. I didn't require it at that moment because, historically, a very high percentage of folks who do not complete ACSC get promoted to Lieutenant Colonel, which was my goal. Part of the lesson I learned in that experience was that when you try to do everything, but everything doesn't benefit you, you will get burned and burned out. You must weigh the risks and benefits in your pursuit of "things" especially as you advance in your career because you just won't have time to waste on things that won't propel you forward.

Time is the one commodity you cannot replace. You will never get time back. So for me, I decided not to complete coursework that didn't serve me well at that time. Today, when I mentor people, I recommend they do whatever it takes to complete that very same coursework because it could be a discriminator later. Still, at that time, I needed to decide to not do something or say no to something where my time and energy were best served elsewhere. Later, I completed the follow-up coursework called Air War College and sacrificed a lot of sleep and free time to get it done. Still, with that, I have set myself up for the benefits that only course completion will afford me. I don't plan on "leaving anything else on the table."

Now, fast forward to a situation that affects my present day. I am currently doing certificate coursework in physician leadership, and it is prerequisite coursework for a master's in business administration in medical management. The certificate coursework is excellent and gives me many tools for my work and what I hope to do in the future, but the certificate itself may not be widely recognized. An MBA, however, is widely recognized and would be great should I decide to be a Chief Medical Officer or Chief Executive Officer at a civilian hospital. It's one of those things where experience in the field may be great, but experiential expertise plus education has to be better, right?

I can once again further my education at minimal-to-no additional cost, but I am hesitant. I am reading a book by Nathalie Molina Niño called Leap Frog. It is the best and most useful entrepreneurial self-help book I have read. In it, she describes an exercise she uses with the entrepreneurs she mentors, and I will tell you about it verbatim here.

'I ask them to close their eyes. "Imagine you've not just launched your business but seen it become wildly successful beyond anything you could have imagined. You've achieved your dreams. Now, in this world you have created, picture yourself waking up in the morning." Then I ask them to walk me through a whole day—not a perfect day of today or tomorrow but one in the world where their dreams have come true—by asking a series of questions: What are you having for breakfast? Is somebody with you in bed? Where are you waking up? Are you on a tropical island? Are you in the middle of Manhattan? Do you have kids? What's the first thing you're going to do? Are you going to go to an office or not? When we're done, we look at their dream day and the business they're building and can usually see pretty quickly if they can coexist.'

This exercise can work for anyone and in any situation if you tweak the questions a bit. I had never considered anything like this exercise, but it was groundbreaking because while I do not have all the answers to the questions worked out, a few things are crystal clear—after I make it big or retire from this first job of mine, I will not work a 9-to-5, I want an abbreviated schedule, I want to have the freedom to work from any part of the globe— high priority will be tropical islands, I will wake without an alarm, I want to be immersed in the love of my husband, kids, and family, and I want to be able to slow down and not be consumed by the stress that rushes me.

I know no hospital Chief Medical Officer (CMO) or Chief Executive Officer (CEO) with the schedule and freedom I have described. If I find that, that will be my work but until then…CMO and CEO don't fit my future workflow and life. So then, why would I spend my precious free time now pursuing things to become something that doesn't fit the characteristics of my "dream day"?

For me, the best thing might be to pass on the MBA, which would cost time studying, time away from my kids, and the fun activities I like to do, like sleep, travel, and attending curated social events. Instead, I can get all the on-the-job experience from my current work and then add some DIY business school information to fill the gaps and become a consultant or coach.

But do you see how easy it is to get lost in pursuit? If you are not intimately in tune with your goal, "your why," and your future desires, then it can be easy for you to get caught up in collecting things that won't ultimately benefit you. Yes, do all the things that bring you joy and all the professional pursuits that make sense. But you have to make them make sense in your life. The only way to reorient yourself is to shift back to your why, your purpose, your perfect day.

Don't get off track.

# NOTES

## CHAPTER TEN

# TIME

"There are two ways of meeting difficulties: you alter the difficulties or you alter yourself meeting them" - Phyllis Bottome

## Do you know the value of your time?

After graduating from college, I went to Texas for military training. At the training's completion, it was time for me to move from Texas to Virginia for my first duty assignment, and my dad came out to take the drive with me. My dad is retired, so he has access to Space Available (Space-A or military hops) Flights, which are rides on military planes at a very low cost. Usually, though, what you gain with low price, you lose in convenience because you are flying standby at the mercy of a trip itinerary catered to others. Also, your military status, i.e., retired, reserve, or active duty, play a role in your priority to get on the plane, with active duty being the highest priority. So the plan was for my dad to fly to Texas on a hop, ride with me to Virginia, and then take a military hop from Virginia back to California.

The first two legs of the trip went without a hitch, but the last leg proved more difficult. It was summer, so my dad didn't have a tight schedule but had a hard stop date for his annual summer trip with my mom. We could not get him on a flight in Virginia, so he had to travel north to Washington, D.C. He was able to get out from there, but it took him to some other location, only to be stranded there and pushed up against his timeline. So, from there, he had to rent a car and buy a commercial flight to make it home in time. He had a similar story when he went to the Olympics in Georgia, Obama's first inauguration, and when he attempted to make the Olympics in Sidney, Australia. He consistently spent more money on the trip than if he had gone the traditional route and booked commercial flights.

My dad also spent too many years working on his own vehicles and still drives several miles, at times to neighboring towns even, to get a deal on gas. He is frugal, and his do-it-yourself mentality, even if it meant wasting a lot of time trying to do something cheaper, rubbed off on me heavily.

I started doing my own hair when I was in elementary school. Routine visits to the hair salon weren't in my budget until well after my first job. I don't like car payments, and I usually undercut personal care that requires maintenance. While at my first military training in Texas, I thought I might start changing my own oil and transmission fluid regularly, but after that first transmission fluid exchange, I resolved that I should leave that to the experts. I am also that person who used to get too much confidence watching HGTV and think I could renovate my entire home in 60 days.

I can do anything; in the past, my default was to try everything myself. Usually, that would result in me getting halfway through something and then realizing that I had no desire to keep going and either leaving an unfinished project or hiring someone to do it.

When I think about doing a project around the house, for example, I think about the cost, and then I weigh my ability to do it myself. Most recently, I wanted an accent wall installed in our bedroom. I did not like the estimates I received, so I watched multiple videos on YouTube, measured, and mapped out our bedroom wall. Then I went to the Lowes and put all the necessary items in my cart. I spent about two hours with a full cart looking at everything and rethinking how this project would turn out. It had disaster written all over it, so I returned everything to their appropriate locations and walked out of the store.

I finally learned my lesson about D-I-Y activities. I am not about that life, and paying the right people to do what I want to be done makes more sense because my time is limited and, therefore, valuable.

If you were to take the amount of money you make in one year from all your sources of income and divide that by the average number of full-time hours worked in a year, 2,080, you would then know your hourly rate for your expertise. The average person works 40 hours weekly for 52 weeks, equating to 2,080 hours per year. This number will give you a reasonable estimate, but if you want to get even more specific, you can subtract free holidays and your vacation and sick time. So, now that you have that number let's think conceptually about overtime. I don't qualify for overtime, but most overtime pays time and a half, i.e., 1.5 times your standard pay rate, because it is understood that your free time is valuable. You should be compensated extra if someone wants you to work during your allotted off time, paying you a convenience fee to incentivize your work during this valuable time. I know your free time is "valuable" to you, but now, I want you to assign a dollar amount to it. This is very important because once you know the value of your free time, you can make many decisions easier. In Jessica Greene's article on zapier.com titled What Is Your Time Really Worth? She says, "What I've learned through this process is the benefit of thinking of all of your time in terms of hourly rates. It can make a lot of decisions easier: Should you take the train or drive? Hire someone to paint your house or do it yourself? Order through Uber Eats or pick up take-out? Hire a virtual assistant or do the work yourself? Invest in a new tool or do the work manually?"

I only started to change my mindset about time a few years ago. I've learned there are many ways to earn money, but once time is lost, there is no getting it back. More plainly stated, even money lost can be returned, but time lost is lost forever. With everything I am doing, from work to hobbies and all the people I am responsible for and the family time I hold dear, time is my most valued commodity, and I will take extreme measures to protect it. I don't allow people to waste my time, and I scrutinize my time down to the minute.

I don't work for myself, and most people don't, so we rarely have total control of every second of our day, but while in pursuit of complete control of all our time, we can settle for abject control of the time we have power over plus the ability to demand the appropriate compensation for our free time. Once you do this exercise, you should have good information to conceptually understand the value of your time, making it easier for you to decide whether you should do something versus paying someone to do it for you. Ultimately this would allow you to offload tasks and free up your time.

I recently came across and completed the "Value of Your Time Calculator" activity on clearerthinking.org, and I would highly recommend that you do it as well. The assessment highlighted one area that I know still reins true: that despite all that I wrote above, I continue to have the mindset of doing things myself and that I genuinely need to internalize the worth of my time.

After we had our fourth child, one of the most significant decisions we made was to join the Au Pair program. The Au Pair Program is one of many state government cultural exchange programs where a person from another country lives with you while providing childcare. We knew we needed more help long ago and considered having an Au Pair or a Nanny. However, we were often deterred by the perceived cost, privacy, security of candidates, the process, or just thinking we were okay to do it alone. We eventually decided to try it with the thought that if we didn't like it, we could just complete the year and never do it again. This was one of the best decisions that offloaded so much for us, and we gained so much in return. As a couple, we are outnumbered by children, and the extra set of hands is glorious. Also, the cultural exchange is great for our children, and we opt to choose Au Pairs from Spanish-speaking countries because two of our children are bilingual, which is an added benefit. Finally, we get to incorporate dedicated date nights, which has allowed me and my husband to spend regular time together, strengthening our relationship.

We have not found a regular house cleaner, but that will be next. When not sketchy, Task Rabbit helps with things like putting furniture together, organizing, or painting. I did paint a bathroom and hang shelves recently, but that was because the Taskers kept trying to change the schedule or cancel on me. Ultimately, I would like to hire a personal assistant, and I think I can afford it- I may just need to cut back on some of my personal shopping to make it happen.

I mentioned before that I don't regularly visit a hair salon, and I also do the hair of my two girls, so that is three heads of hair that I am responsible for. There are multiple reasons, not just associated with cost, as to why we all don't go to the salon. But it highlights another thing I should mention. Sometimes we can get in our heads about the cost of a service, not realizing that paying someone to do a task for us frees up time to either earn more, advance a project that could lead to more return, or allows us to rest and recuperate to then reenergize for life's demands. I can get stuck on thoughts like, should I pay for this now in hopes of making more money, or should I wait to make more money to be able to pay for this service?

Well, I am here to tell you, "Stop it!" Get out of your head. Make that investment and free up your time to do whatever you want with it.

# NOTES

## CHAPTER ELEVEN

# BETTER

"The best preparation for tomorrow is doing your best today." - H. Jackson Brown, Jr.

I have a husband, four children, and an Au Pair living at home. I used to be the primary cook, planning all the meals and cooking after I commuted for an hour from work. My husband previously said he did not like to cook and only occasionally participated in the cooking. That started when we only had two or three children and no Au Pair, but this became an unreasonable setup, and we began to share the work with me, still cooking on most weekdays.

Now we do things differently. Our two oldest children are 13 and 11 and are old enough to participate in meals, so our cooking schedule looks like this:

Mondays, our 13-year-old cooks,
Tuesdays, the Au Pair cooks,
Wednesdays, I cook,
Thursdays, our 11-year-old son cooks,
Fridays, I cook,
Saturdays and Sundays, my husband cooks.

Household chores are also divided amongst the two eldest children, and the Au Pair helps out. I have created an operating instruction for the kitchen that includes instructions on how to do things like washing the dishes and divides the work into two- and three-person teams.

I have thought about creating videos of how to do things the way I like them done because having an au pair has taught me that not everyone does things the same way. Social media is a good enough example to affirm that all people don't prepare their food the same, take the same food safety precautions, wash dishes the same, or even sort and wash and fold clothes the same. And "the same" isn't actually what I mean. People just don't do things the way I want them to be done.

Our operation only partially alleviates my stress about house maintenance, upkeep, and division of duties. Still, it means that the burden of work isn't just on my shoulders, and sometimes I get a few moments to do other things or other chores that need to be done.

A simple term for this is delegation.

I need a lot of work in employing this in my professional life.

I am the person who subconsciously says I can do it faster, more reliably, and of course, my way if I do the work independently. I don't have to worry about running ideas by other individuals, teaching skills, or succumbing to another person's way of doing something for the sake of compromise. But this way of thinking does not make me effective at getting the massive amount of work done that is involved with being a mother who manages the household, a physician leader, and an entrepreneur while also doing the other things that I love, like serving at my church, exploring our city, attending events, and traveling the world. And, by the way, I don't want to give up any of these things.

In 2005, Roderick and I founded Leaders Inspiring Fruitful Tomorrows, also known as LIFT. It is a 501(c)(3) nonprofit charitable organization dedicated to providing mentoring opportunities to minority, traditionally underserved, and first-generation youth interested in going to college. We create opportunities for early exposure to professional persons of color in STEM (and other) career fields. We build relationships with students through frequent mentoring and guidance. We create opportunities for students and their parents to learn and create a financial plan for education. We introduce and develop soft skills in children to create professional leaders who can think critically. In 17 years, we have been minimally effective in our mission statements year after year. I have attempted to do all the work and have only seen gains when I have allowed others to participate in the vision or others have advocated for us and created spaces for us to grow and expand. Running a nonprofit, especially through a pandemic and recession, means that most of the time, you are checking your bank account to see if you have enough to fund your operating expenses for another year. Then you are constantly considering what budget items you can cut to ensure your most effective programs keep running. Regarding LIFT, money and time are our most precious commodities, but what are either without great leadership?

A delegating leadership style is a low-task approach where a leader empowers an individual to exercise autonomy. In this approach, you provide individuals with the big picture and entrust them with delivering agreed-upon results. Using our nonprofit as an example, I have failed to utilize our board of directors and other resources to their fullest potential- creating a unified vision and allowing them to work within their areas of strength and expertise to produce deliverables that push our organization forward but also, allow us to simply, lead.

I could use this in my clinical leadership as well. But this has become difficult in medicine as short staffing in clinical spaces translates to leaders who become doers more often than they are allowed to lead. This is problematic because when all the leaders become the doers, you lose leadership, strategic and operational progress. Leaders need to be able to lead. They have a unique skill that is best served where leaders lead, not in the trenches. I don't know if this practice of multi-hatting clinicians is something that occurs in sectors outside of medicine, but I am pretty sure no one would ask a pilot to fuel the plane before he hops in to fly it. Still, I see our clinical leaders being plucked from their leadership roles to fill in to keep operations flowing. It is a disservice to their specialized training and valuable input at "the table"…okay, enough of that soap box.

The critical lesson I am learning as I write this is that I need to be a better delegator to take my leadership to the next level.

As I read more and learn about the constructs of an effective board of directors, I plan to change the construct of our board and their roles and responsibilities, increase our meeting intervals, and incorporate proven methodology to increase our productivity.

Delegation is a crucial aspect of effective leadership and plays a significant role in building strong leaders. It involves assigning tasks, responsibilities, and decision-making authority to team or organization members. Here are some key reasons why delegation is important in leadership:

1. Focus on core responsibilities: Delegation allows leaders to concentrate on their core responsibilities and strategic initiatives. By transferring routine or less critical tasks to others, leaders can invest their time and energy in high-level decision-making, problem-solving, and vision setting, which are crucial for the organization's success.

2. Development of team members: Delegation allows leaders to foster their team members' growth and development. By assigning tasks aligned with their skills, interests, and developmental goals, leaders empower individuals to take on new challenges, enhance their expertise, and build self-confidence. Delegating tasks also promotes cross-training and knowledge sharing within the team, leading to a more skilled and versatile workforce. A key point here is to know enough about your people to know their interests and strengths. Coming from a person who has had many tasks delegated to them, there have been occasions where jobs had no developmental link. Sometimes I will still take those jobs, depending on the situation and my availability.

3. Building trust and accountability: Delegation demonstrates trust in the abilities of team members and fosters a sense of ownership and accountability. When leaders delegate tasks, they communicate that they believe in their team's capabilities and are willing to share responsibility. This trust-building aspect of

delegation strengthens the bond between leaders and team members, enhances motivation, and encourages individuals to take the initiative and perform at their best.

4. Promoting teamwork and collaboration: Delegation encourages collaboration and teamwork within a group. When leaders delegate tasks, team members must collaborate, share information, and coordinate their efforts. This promotes a collaborative culture, fosters effective communication, and enhances the overall cohesiveness within the team. Strong leaders understand the value of collaboration and leverage delegation to create a cohesive and high-performing team.

5. Developing leadership skills: Delegation allows leaders to develop and refine their own leadership skills. By entrusting others with tasks, leaders can practice coaching, mentoring, and guiding their team. They can also enhance their ability to provide constructive feedback, align individual strengths with organizational goals, and create an environment encouraging learning and growth. Through delegation, leaders learn to be more adaptable, flexible, and skilled in managing diverse talents.

6. Ensuring continuity and scalability: Delegation is crucial for building resilient organizations that can sustain growth and adapt to change. When leaders delegate tasks, they distribute knowledge and decision-making authority across the team, reducing reliance on a single person. This ensures continuity even without

the presence of a leader and allows the organization to scale its operations effectively. Delegation empowers leaders to build a strong leadership pipeline by identifying and nurturing future leaders within the team.

Delegation is vital for effective leadership and the development of strong leaders. It allows leaders to focus on strategic initiatives, promotes the growth of team members, and ensures organizational continuity.

As a physician leader, I plan to utilize my teams more effectively and empower individuals by creating the space for them to work and grow in their areas of expertise. By doing less of the doing and more of the clearing, leading, and provisioning, I want to create a dynamic and empowered team that drives success and achieves meaningful goals.

More important than becoming a better, more humble leader, I hope these implementations will strengthen teams around me, prepare others to lead beside me, improve my ability to use my creativity to propel these businesses, and free up time, physical, and mental energy for me to do me. This is the mastery of being better I aim to achieve.

# NOTES

# CHAPTER TWELVE

# REWRITTEN

"As I walked out the door toward the gate that would lead to my freedom, I knew if I didn't leave my bitterness and hatred behind, I'd still be in prison." - Nelson Mandela

I have kept in touch with a group of friends I met at Tuskegee University through ROTC, and we have a group chat. We recently had a meetup video conference, and it was so good to catch up and see their faces and get a glimpse of their spouses or children as they stopped by to chat with us. On that call, I confessed to my friends that I was bitter about my experience at Tuskegee. And they questioned me as to why. I have shared this comment with a couple in close circles but have never really talked about why I feel that way. Still, I am bitter to the point where it has prevented me from returning for homecoming, donating funds, and until recently, wearing my school paraphernalia even though I graduated from the illustrious Tuskegee University, a Historically Black College or University (HBCU).

I grew up in Sacramento, California, and because my dad was the original helicopter dad, I decided to go far away to attend college. To pursue my dream of becoming a doctor, my next choice during high school was to determine where I would attend college. I was set on getting as far away from my dad as possible. I first settled on Michigan State University (MSU) but was also accepted with a small scholarship to Tuskegee University. Despite my plan to attend MSU, my dad was thrilled at the idea of me attending Tuskegee University and bargained with me to do a campus visit. I had visited neither campus. So, we went to Tuskegee, Alabama, by way of Atlanta, Georgia. I was immediately taken aback by the beauty of Tuskegee's campus and the proximity to my cousin in Atlanta, Georgia. Apparently, I love the look of brick and sunshine and the humidity of the south, so I accepted the offer to attend Tuskegee University.

Moving to Alabama and attending an HBCU was a complete culture shock, but I loved it. Socially, I became a cheerleader, later joined ROTC, and then spent my last two years as a member of the P-I-P, E-R-E, double T-E-S, the Piperettes." A Piperette is the elite dance team that performs with the band- The Marching Piper Band during football halftime shows. I want you to look that up if you have no idea what I am talking about because if you have never seen a halftime performance by an HBCU band, you are in for an experience. Academically, I also did well.
So where does the bitterness come from?

I can put my frustrations into three categories: Environment, Academics, and Relationships.

Tuskegee University is located in Tuskegee, Alabama, and is similar to many colleges in small towns. Its closest cities of interest are Montgomery and Auburn, Alabama, and Tuskegee is roughly 2 hours from Atlanta, Georgia. When I speak of the environment, the literal proximity to nothing has little to do with my gripes. I am referencing the accommodations and the upkeep of the facilities, classrooms, etc. My first dorm room was in Adam's Hall, and it was located very central to the campus- right next door to the cafeteria and the central hub for socializing, which is affectionately called "The Yard." The room was typical dorm style, with two mirrored sides for me and my roommate and communal bathrooms and showers at the end of the hall. There was a common area on the other end of the hall that people could use for studying in groups or watching television. Adam's Hall was where I was first introduced to thumb and finger-sized roaches. We had a seating area outside the dorm where we would sit and hold court, and the cockroaches would hang with the best of us. There was also a huge hole in the ceiling due to missing and damaged ceiling tiles right outside the bathroom entrance, and giant roaches would hang out on the wall there. The lighting in and just outside the bathroom was shoddy, so it was dimly lit. Alabama roaches are enormous, bold, and undeterred, so a journey to the bathroom for a shower often included running, ducking, jumping, and squealing. Other things made college life interesting, like the trek to wash clothes, the lack of facilities within our respective colleges to study, and the failure of faculty and staff to know how to mentor effectively in our desired career fields, for me that was specifically medicine.

Specific to my area of study, we did not have access to medical college admissions test prep coursework or a location to take the test on campus, so we had to travel to Auburn to take the classes and to also take the test; many of us without transportation to make that happen; so, therefore, we had to barter and beg because there were no affordable transportation options to get there otherwise. This is partly attributable to my lack of research into what would make a good college experience for me and what college would be a good fit for my desired career, but also a testament to the limitations of being accepted to a small number of colleges and the desire to go out of state.

I expected that college would be educationally challenging in a manner that would prepare me for medical college admissions testing and medical school. I was ill-advised as a person wanting to be a doctor to change my major from chemical engineering to biology. As a biology major, I became part of the College of Agriculture, Environment, and Nutrition Sciences (CAENS), where Tuskegee sticks close to its roots in focusing on agricultural sciences. I did not find any focus on students who were interested in becoming physicians, and there was technically no pre-medicine curriculum. Once again, my lack of preparedness in this regard is noted.

During my time in college, I had the opportunity to meet some truly remarkable individuals who have become invaluable friends. Concurrently, I gained valuable experience discerning suitable partners for intimate relationships, as I encountered numerous individuals who failed to meet my expectations. Through those relationships, I learned to value myself and recognize people with ill intent or who could not meet my relational standards. But if I were to run into anyone I dated in the past, say at homecoming or the supermarket, there is no telling how I might react. Closure doesn't necessarily mean freedom from past hurt or anger.

I could quickly speak about all the above when discussing Mother Tuskegee's shortcomings. However, despite everything I mentioned that occurred to me then and everything else I choose not to say, I emerged resilient, bold, and undeterred by most external environments. I became a physician who made it despite what I perceived was missing from my education or the resources available to me in college. I am also in a healthy relationship with a loving and supportive partner.

It was destined for me to have those experiences so that I could grow and become who I am today.

Tony Schwartz, Chief Executive Officer of The Energy Project and author of The Way We're Working Isn't Working and Catherine McCarthy, Senior Vice President at The Energy Project, put it this way:

*People can cultivate positive emotions by learning to change the stories they tell themselves about the events in their lives. Often, people in conflict cast themselves in the role of victim, blaming others or external circumstances for their problems. Becoming aware of the difference between facts in a given situation and the way we interpret those facts can be powerful in itself. It's been a revelation for many of the people we work with to discover they have a choice about how to view a given event and to recognize how powerfully the story they tell influences the emotions they feel. We teach them to tell the most hopeful and personally empowering story possible in any given situation, without denying or minimizing the facts.*

*They go on to advise:*

*The most effective way people can change a story is to view it through any of three new lenses, which are all alternatives to seeing the world from the victim perspective. With the reverse lens, for example, people ask themselves, "What would the other person in this conflict say and in what ways might that be true?" With the long lens they ask, "How will I most likely view this situation in six months?" With the wide lens they ask themselves,*

*"Regardless of the outcome of this issue, how can I grow and learn from it?" Each of these lenses can help people intentionally cultivate more positive emotions.*

I am certainly not a victim, and every experience I have had was necessary to shape my success. However, I never realized the victim mentality I assumed when discussing my college experiences. As such, I do not want to portray my college experience in that manner, and with the *reverse lens,* I acknowledge the necessary research and considerations when it comes to choosing the right college. I tell my mentees that they need to research schools with vital programs in their desired career fields and all the supporting extracurricular activities and facilities that make a program strong and innovative to make the learning experience rewarding. Second, they should focus on location and amenities. In my *long lens*, which is now, I should have never harbored these feelings for so long. Finally, with a wide lens, I am cognizant of all the life lessons I learned from my experiences at Tuskegee University. I will forever write my story as this:

I attended a beautiful Historical Black College with a rich history that began with the education of Black Americans who had limited means to become educated then. I was stretched environmentally, academically, and emotionally as most are when they leave home for college. I owe my success and my successful relationships to the experiences that I had at Tuskegee University.

Moreover, attending Tuskegee University was a truly enriching experience on multiple levels. The campus exuded a sense of history and significance, reminding me of the incredible individuals who came before me and their strides in pursuing education and equality. This backdrop served as a constant reminder of the importance of perseverance, resilience, and the power of education.

My time at Tuskegee University was not just about earning a degree but about immersing myself in an environment that empowered me to grow academically, emotionally, and socially. The memories, friendships, and transformative experiences I gained during those years will forever be cherished, and I am immensely proud to write my story as one that is intertwined with the rich legacy of Tuskegee University.

This thought transformation was especially hard for me because finding the positive in negative experiences is heavily linked to forgiveness, and the inability to easily forgive is one of my toxic traits. It requires a willingness to let go of resentment, anger, and the desire for revenge, which can be deeply rooted and difficult to overcome. It is essential to understand that forgiveness is not about condoning or forgetting the hurt caused by others or the circumstances we have faced. Instead, it is a conscious choice to release ourselves from those negative emotions and allow ourselves to heal and move forward.

An older woman in her seventies or eighties frequently sat beside us at church. She shared a lot with us, including details about her husband and his illness, and we enjoyed sitting next to her and hearing her stories about her family and her resiliency. We would text her to check on her when she missed a service, and she was on our mailing list for our annual Christmas card during the holidays. One day, she shared that her sister's child, her niece, had died when the child was very young. Their mother, the child's grandmother, was sitting for her and had put her in her crib to sleep. As our friend described, back then, you let children "cry it out," and so the mother never checked on the child. Eventually, the child stopped crying. The child, however, had gotten wedged on the side of the crib and could not free herself. She died while in the care of her grandmother.

The family was devastated.

Can you imagine?

The guilt and shame of that grandmother. The anger and hurt of the mother and father. The trauma of the entire family.

Now and then, I think about this story, especially when my children were very young. And when I thought about it, first, it would be in instructing a caregiver that "we don't 'cry it out' in this house," secondly, I wondered how I might have reacted in that situation. Would I be able to forgive and rewrite that story to salvage the relationship with my mother and do further works to help heal my family?

I hope never to know a situation like that, but I do know that this woman forgave her mother.

You, too, have the ownership rights to your story. We cannot control what happens in our lives, but we can manage the aftermath. Embrace the idea that you have the power to reinterpret those experiences and extract meaningful lessons from them. To rewrite your story and release yourself from the constraints of negativity, it is essential to first recognize that your past does not define you. Each experience, whether positive or negative, has contributed to your growth and shaped who you are today.

No matter how devastating a situation, reflect on the narrative you have been telling yourself and identify any recurring patterns or negative beliefs that have held you back. Challenge these beliefs by reframing them in a more empowering light. Instead of seeing yourself as a victim of circumstances, view yourself as a resilient individual who has overcome challenges and emerged stronger.

I know this is all easier said than done, but we still have to do it.

I would never minimize the magnitude of the effects of the events of anyone's past, but we still must work through it.

Taking ownership of your story involves accepting responsibility for your emotions, choices, and actions and the effect other people's actions have had on you. Recognize that you can choose how you respond to challenging situations and how you shape your future. Use your past experiences as stepping stones towards personal growth and positive transformation.

The tragic story of the loss suffered by this woman's family highlights the immense power of forgiveness in overcoming great wrongs. My struggles during college pale in comparison, but they constitute some of my life's biggest challenges.

Empathy, resilience, and a commitment to personal growth are essential to navigate such profound circumstances. Grounding oneself in the wisdom of Nelson Mandela's words, embracing our duty to forgive, and drawing upon past triumphs can provide strength. Forgiveness then becomes a courageous and transformative act, rewriting the narrative of the past and fostering healing and reconciliation for all involved.

And if this is still too difficult for you, you and I can continue to work on our execution of forgiveness by keeping the ball rolling, forgiving what we can, and rewriting our stories, one at a time.

# NOTES

## CHAPTER THIRTEEN
# ROCK

"We build our life on the hope for tomorrow, yet tomorrow brings us closer to death and is the ultimate enemy; people live their lives as if they were not aware of the certainty of death." - Albert Camus

My purpose was to become a physician who used that platform as a leaping board into physician leadership, medical professional development, and clinical quality and safety. Only from that platform, with all the education, training, and experience, was I able to use that platform to inspire and lead children to change their communities through college education. And through all that, I was purposed to be half of a whole marriage and raise four children to impart their gifts to the world. This is crystal clear to me now, but it has occurred to me that some people don't believe in the idea of purpose and purposeful living. Instead, they think life has no meaning, and our lives are filled with meaningless activities.

This can be illustrated through the character Sisyphus. In Greek mythology, Sisyphus is a figure best known for his punishment of pushing a boulder up a hill only to have it roll back down and repeat the process for eternity. The exact crimes for which

Sisyphus was punished are not explicitly stated; however, his deceitful and arrogant nature is emphasized historically. He was known for his cunning trickery and was believed to have deceived mortals and gods alike. He cheated death, once by tricking Hades, the god of the underworld, into releasing him from the realm of the dead, and another time by convincing Persephone, Hades' wife, to let him return to the world of the living. It has also been suggested that he generally disregarded the gods and their laws. Sisyphus was also believed to have committed various other crimes and immoral acts.

The story of Sisyphus has been interpreted in many ways throughout history. One interpretation is that it represents the futility of human existence, as humans are often forced to engage in repetitive or meaningless tasks that ultimately lead nowhere. Another interpretation is that it represents the consequences of arrogance and deceit, as Sisyphus was punished for his dishonesty and was forced to engage in a task that was impossible to complete.

The 20th-century philosopher, Albert Camus, wrote an essay titled "The Myth of Sisyphus," in which he explored the philosophical implications of the story. He argued that Sisyphus represents the absurdity of human existence, as we are forced to engage in meaningless tasks and ultimately face our own mortality. His interpretation of the situation of Sisyphus is part of his 'philosophy of the absurd,' which is a juxtaposition between the fundamental human need to attribute meaning to life and the 'unreasonable silence' of the universe in response.

At first glance, you might think that Albert Camus has a problem with God and purposeful living, but his philosophical debate seems to be much more than that. His deduction of life's unknowns and unanswered questions fuels his philosophy on absurdity and a life that ultimately has no meaning.

While this was an interesting aside, I return to Sisyphus and his devotion to pushing a boulder up a hill. Some might see the labor of Sisyphus as pointless because it undoes itself every day, resulting in no progress or success. I prefer Chhavi Kumar's, a writer for Medium, approach to the topic, which contradicts what Camus believed. In the realm of Sisyphus and his eternal task, Kumar's perspective offers a fascinating departure from the conventional interpretation. Instead of dismissing Sisyphus's labor as futile, she imbues it with profound significance, regarding the rock as a symbol of his purpose. In this view, the boulder represents an unending struggle and a constant reminder of Sisyphus's dedication and resilience.

The idea of purpose being permanent brings forth a thought-provoking notion that purpose, once discovered, endures beyond the bounds of time. While Camus might have viewed the task as an absurd and meaningless endeavor, Kumar's interpretation allows us to explore the importance of perseverance and determination. The continuous push for improvement and progress becoming an art, with the eventual manifestation of beauty in life as its ultimate reward.

In applying this concept to our own lives, we, too, can find meaning in our pursuits and endeavors. The process becomes as crucial as the outcome, emphasizing the journey rather than the destination. We can then open ourselves to the idea that our efforts contribute to a greater purpose, no matter how arduous or repetitive. It encourages us to find beauty and fulfillment in striving, creating a profound shift in how we perceive and engage with life's challenges. In a world where success is often measured by final achievements, this alternative perspective breathes new life into the timeless tale of Sisyphus, urging us to redefine success and embrace the significance of our individual journeys. Camus' essay concludes, "The struggle itself … is enough to fill a man's heart. One must imagine Sisyphus happy". One assumption that must be made is that Sisyphus did not have the option to walk away from his rock. It was his punishment to push the rock up the hill no matter how many times it rolled down. The idea of purpose is quite similar. While being created with a purpose, the only failure would be not living in your own purpose. As such, once your purpose is known, you are obligated to work and be the best at your purpose, no matter the challenges you may face. If you hit a roadblock that delays your progression, you must either find your way through or build a way around that obstacle. If you feel like you are failing, fail forward- find something in that experience that you can use as a lesson to propel you forward.

The COVID-19 Pandemic introduced me to "living in the moment" and "living my life to the fullest." I became pregnant in 2019 with my fourth child, and he was delivered right in the middle of the pandemic. This was a terribly heartbreaking time for many who lost loved ones, employment, and hope in humanity. On the other side, though, there was much revelation about the value of life and the active daily participation in life as it relates to career, family, and support for others. Not only did I create life during that time, but I also went through an awakening that forced me to stop waiting to do things meant for me. I wanted to renew my language study, so I began taking Spanish with a tutor in Costa Rica. I loved to travel, but it always seemed like something was going on in my life that prohibited it from happening, whether it was pregnancy or just not wanting to disrupt the flow of our family's lives. But, in 2021, I went on a trip with my sister and niece to Belize to celebrate my birthday, and I had an amazing time. The following year, I threw myself a themed party, which I had wanted to do for so long. Today, I rarely pass up an opportunity to do something that I think would be fun- like going to Coachella or Diner en Blanc. I love a unique or curated experience; just look up what Diner en Blanc entails if you have never heard of it. Knowing what activities I find enjoyable and the times of the day I like to be 'outside' makes it easy for me to say no to activities that don't add to my happiness. In addition to curated social events, I like timeless clothing, selfie museums, traveling, spending time with family, professional photography, the smell of honeysuckle, and gourmet vegan gummy bears sans artificial colors and flavors.

What about you? Do you know your purpose? Or what things bring you happiness? Where do you find your joy?

Worse than not being able to do the things you love regularly is a blank stare because you haven't figured it out yet.

If that is you, do me a favor and take some time to think about your answers to those questions because pushing along your rock will be so much easier when you surround it with the beautiful things and experiences that make life joyful for you.

# NOTES

## CHAPTER FOURTEEN

# WHOLE

Good morning,

I am Dr. Tarra Faulk. I am the Chief of the Nephrology department, where Sergeant [--] worked for the past year.

It is with great sadness that we gather today. If you knew the character and work ethic of Technical Sergeant (TSgt) [--], then you know we could have easily been here with him, celebrating an award or an honor. Instead, we have come to honor his life while reflecting on his death.

I first met Sergeant [--] about a year ago. He was out on the dialysis floor joking and laughing with the staff and patients while going through his training.

There was one thing about Sergeant [--] that you could not miss and that was his size. When I saw him for the first time I thought: who is this very buff guy and does he work out all day?

I immediately felt like I needed to go to the gym.

Despite his size, [any] friend would accurately describe him as a gentle giant.

I immediately knew by the way that he interacted with our unique [and complex] patient population that he would be a perfect match for our section.

He quickly became a part of our family.

He had an infectious personality and was an experienced leader.

I often overheard him mentoring airmen and young [Noncomissioned Officers] NCOs [well after our last patients had left.]

TSgt [--] was missed during his six-month deployment and we eagerly awaited his return.

My last contact with him was over email. He sent me his [Enlisted Performance Report] EPR bullets and congratulated my family for the pending birth of my daughter.

When she was born, I didn't bother to send him pictures because I figured I would see him [when I returned to work.]

I took for granted that I could show him in person when we both returned to work.

Some of you may have had similar plans. There would be stories told of all the crazy things that occurred in his absence, great pictures to show him, and laughs to be shared, all when he returned.

Sergeant [--] performed well on his deployment and had plans to [Permanently Change Station] PCS to Turkey in the Spring. We were happy for him because he was excited. We expected to lose him, but never in this manner.

I'm sure we are all distraught by the circumstances surrounding his death. In the days following his passing, we have experienced a mixture of emotions: grief, anger, emptiness, sorrow, numb[ness], raw, regret, guilt, denial, and disbelief.

I, like many of you, am not okay and I continue to try to process what TSgt [--] may have been going through.

I never saw this coming.

You may wonder if and how you missed something, or whether you could have intervened, and that is normal.

You may have similar or different feelings whether you personally knew TSgt [--] or not and that is okay too. It is okay to mourn this situation and the loss.

My plea, to you all, is that you don't struggle through this alone. Now more than ever we must stand in community and lean on our wingman for support. Together we can be made stronger through any situation. We are fortunate to be part of an organization with an abundance of resources to help prevent desperation. Get to know what resources are available now so that you can be prepared in your time of need.

Though it may seem like we are surrounded by darkness, as it is written in the Holy Bible, the book of Luke, chapter 1, verses 78-79: ...the morning light from heaven is about to break upon us, to give light to those who sit in darkness and in the shadow of death, and to guide us to the path of peace. It is my hope that we all find peace as we mourn our dear colleague and friend.

Shortly after I spoke these words in front of TSgt [--]'s family, our colleagues, and friends, I returned to work after being out of the office for 12 weeks following the birth of my third child. His death was initially thought to be an apparent suicide, but much later, it was determined that, instead, it was an accidental lethal combination of alcohol and pain medications.

A short while later, I watched as the life left one of my sickest patient's body. He was on hemodialysis in our unit, and my nurses called me in because he looked unwell and wasn't responding. I directed the nursing staff to rinse his blood back into his body, only to watch as his heart stopped beating and the color again left him. As this was happening, I left the room to contact his wife; a woman I had known now for quite some time, but I could not reach her. Finally, she called back to our nurse's station, and I urged her to come and meet me in the dialysis unit. To my surprise, she arrived minutes later, wheeled down from the medical-surgical unit because she was admitted to the hospital. As she was being wheeled back, only then could I tell her that her husband had died. He was entrusted to us. He was so sick. He had asked to not be resuscitated.

Ed Sheeran said that grief instantly ends your youth. He said this when speaking about his friend Jamal Edwards who died of a drug overdose in 2022. While the suffering from grief is meant to be temporary, it still leaves remnants like puzzle pieces that occasionally come together to remind you of the volatile nature of life; it is but a vapor. Suddenly you can be reminded of your resident who died of cancer in her twenties, only six months after her diagnosis; your program director who suffered a massive hemorrhagic stroke while on vacation; your technician who was found dead on his apartment floor; the many patients who were too sick to survive.

At that point, I knew I was not okay. I had TSgt [--]'s memorial program stapled to my desk's bulletin board and saw it every day. None of us understood his death. I replayed every interaction to see if there was an intervenable moment. I found nothing. This continued, and I was still not okay. And so, I scheduled an appointment with behavioral health and the chaplain. I saw the psychologist maybe three times and the chaplain twice, and when I felt better, neither of us thought there was a need to continue. Still, the psychologist felt that I was experiencing symptoms of post-traumatic stress disorder (PTSD) due to those traumatic events.

Healthcare providers may experience trauma due to the death of a patient under their care. Experiencing patient deaths can lead to emotional distress, such as feelings of guilt, helplessness, sadness, and grief, and in some cases, healthcare professionals may develop symptoms of PTSD as a result of the trauma. PTSD symptoms may include intrusive thoughts or memories of the patient's death, avoidance of situations that remind them of the event, and hyperarousal, such as difficulty sleeping or being easily startled.

Similarly, as a leader, when a death occurs in a subordinate, especially if suicide is suspected, the same emotional trauma can occur. And similarly, still, there are other occasions in the care of patients where providers may suffer emotional trauma. A term that can be used to describe this phenomenon is "second victim". The term is most commonly used to describe healthcare professionals who experience emotional trauma following a patient event, such as a patient's death or disability unintentionally caused by a provider or within the hospital system. The concept of the second victim acknowledges that healthcare professionals may experience significant distress as a result of their work and may need support to recover and continue to provide quality care to their patients. I would even go beyond the word "may" and say that this happens almost daily to healthcare providers caring for patients.

When a patient receives a diagnosis, not only do they receive it, but the provider caring for the patient does also. And when a patient dies while in your care, you also experience a part of that. The "second victim" term can be controversial, as it may imply that healthcare professionals experience equivalent emotions or harm to those of the patients and their families; however, the concept acknowledges the importance of supporting the emotional well-being of healthcare professionals as they care for patients during difficult times. Also, admitting that providers can be intimately or peripherally involved and still experience some form of emotional distress.

Other professionals experience similar trauma in their day-to-day lives and work. Military, law enforcement, survivors of mass shootings, etc. are just a few examples. Even television programs are triggering for some. People have traumatic childhoods and experiences that they haven't entirely reconciled, contributing to stress. Add relationships with spouses, friends, and family, the pressures of adulthood, and everything else going on in the world, and it is easy to see how people can feel overwhelmed and defeated, me included. The beautiful thing is this, the stigma surrounding seeking help for mental health reasons has all but vanished, and people are embracing the fact that life is overwhelming and can be daunting at times.

Recently, I sought therapy again because I felt overwhelmed and too easily agitated by daily tasks and interactions, especially with my family and friends. I felt like I needed to have more peace within me in order to continue to be excellent and do things excellently. I also felt I needed more tools to parent successfully, interact with people wholly, and live life more presently. I spend a lot of time thinking and dreaming, and making plans. While I do want to continue to dream and seek challenging professional experiences, I also want to experience memorable moments with my husband and children while being able to put down my work on nights and weekends. I want to achieve that work-life balance that makes me feel whole, not stretched in many directions.

Wholeness, for me, will involve integrating the different experiences that I have had, the death of TSgt [--], patient illness and death, constant reflection, and active participation in my own recovery and healing, as well as the incorporation of the different parts of me that together form and align my purpose in life. This will involve identifying and addressing the areas of imbalance or disconnection, such as unprocessed emotions, unhealthy habits, or unfulfilling relationships in my life. It will also require a more profound sense of self-awareness, self-reflection, and inner peace and calm that I know I am incapable of achieving on my own. It also requires me to put myself first and schedule these appointments with the psychologist and not skip over them when

117

meetings show up on my calendar, or I don't feel like driving across town.

I have been going to these weekly appointments for about two months now, and I feel better after each one. I approach conflict differently, and most importantly, when I tell the psychologist that I don't know how to do something, he provides me with a tool or a thought or guidance to place in my toolbox to help me overcome that feeling.

Wholeness is a deeply personal and subjective experience, but it is something that I want to achieve. It takes a lot to be me and do what I do…to be us and do what we do. However, the only way we can continue on our path and continue to serve is by honoring and recognizing the aspects of ourselves that need help, whether that be a therapist, nutritionist, exercise physiologist, sleep therapist, marriage counselor, house cleaner, etc.

Wholeness involves self-acceptance, emotional well-being, mental clarity, authenticity, meaningful connections, physical health, and spiritual fulfillment. It is an ongoing journey unique to individual needs that should empower you to live authentically, find purpose, and experience a more fulfilling and meaningful existence. In seeking the help you need, you positively affect your life of service while striving to live in alignment with your deepest values, beliefs, and dreams.

If you need help with this, here is an exercise that may help.

A practical exercise to becoming whole involves practicing mindfulness. Mindfulness involves being fully present and aware of the present moment without judgment. It can help you cultivate self-awareness, emotional regulation, and a deeper understanding of yourself.

Here's a simple mindfulness exercise you can try:

1. Find a quiet and comfortable space where you won't be disturbed.

2. Sit or lie down in a relaxed position. Close your eyes if it feels comfortable.

3. Take a few deep breaths, inhaling through your nose and exhaling through your mouth.

4. Shift your attention to your body. Scan from head to toe, noticing any physical sensations or areas of tension. Allow yourself to feel and accept these sensations without trying to change them.

5. Bring your focus to your thoughts and emotions. Observe any thoughts that arise without getting attached to them or judging them. Just let them come and go like passing clouds.

6. Acknowledge your emotions without trying to suppress or amplify them. Allow yourself to feel whatever arises, knowing that emotions are a natural part of being human.

7. As you continue to breathe deeply, imagine a warm, comforting light enveloping you, nurturing and embracing all aspects of yourself.

8.  Practice this exercise for 5-10 minutes daily or whenever you need to reconnect with yourself.

Mindfulness can help you become more attuned to your inner world and develop a deeper sense of wholeness by accepting and integrating all parts of yourself. Over time, this practice can lead to increased self-compassion, inner peace, and a more fulfilling sense of being whole.

# NOTES

## CHAPTER FIFTEEN

# NEXT

"I am the true grapevine, and my Father is the gardener. [2] He cuts off every branch of mine that doesn't produce fruit, and he prunes the branches that do bear fruit so they will produce even more" John 15:1-2 (NLT) Jesus, the True Vine

I only have two legit regrets in my entire life, and they are not traveling heavily in my youth and not speaking up or advocating for myself as a teenager and young adult. The travel part couldn't be changed because I was broke, but the other is more interesting.

I recall a time in elementary school when my parents received a note and phone call from my teacher stating that I talked too much. I don't recall what my parents said about it, but I vividly remember that I stopped speaking in class altogether. Not only did I stop talking socially, but I also retreated from round table reading or any other speaking opportunities in class. I remember it then morphing into the feeling of fear any time I was called upon in school. This lasted throughout elementary school and bled into middle and high school, particularly in academic and leadership roles. Despite being very socially active in gymnastics, cheerleading, and dance, I was rather shy on a personal level.

I had relationships with people in high school where I didn't speak up when I should have, and then fast forward to my time in college which is when I was challenged time after time but lacked the maturity, the courage, or the time to seek out and advocate for change. This occurred in academic situations, personal relationships, and military leadership.

I graduated college and then began attending the required military training necessary for my job, and I wasn't doing well. I was smart, but I had no critical thinking skills, and self-reflection and correction weren't a regular part of my life. I had a tough time during Intelligence Officer school, where I had trouble applying my knowledge to create strategic plans. I also struggled with the fear of public speaking, but because intelligence officers prepare and give a lot of briefings, I got better and better, and even now, my PowerPoint slide game is on point.

But still, I only spoke to express my thoughts if specifically asked, and even when asked, I hesitated, as if my contributions weren't worthy of being heard.

During Aerospace Basic Course, I received the following peer feedback:

"needs to talk more,"
"needs to be more vocal,"
"speak up when you have good ideas because you usually do,"
"speak up, be heard,"
"you need to speak up more, you have a lot of good information,"

"quiet, sometimes your opinions are very helpful and they are always valued. Unless you are giving advice on Mexican Restaurants!"

And yes, I have kept every feedback I have received during my entire career in the military.

I successfully made it through that training and Intelligence Officer school and my time as an Intelligence Officer, starting out apprehensive but thriving once I gained my footing.

During residency (after medical school), when I struggling and barely surviving, something clicked on inside me, and I was forever changed. There is one person who witnessed this transition and mentioned it to me. He was my senior resident during my intern year and later a fellow when I rotated through cardiology. He described me as going from a timid, shy person to a bold, outspoken individual, and I agree with his assessment. The turning point occurred when I decided to stop being the special guest at my own pity party and forcefully try to better everything in my life that was within my control. And from then on, I worked to be a better student, an intentional leader, a better physician, a better mother, a better wife and companion, and a better friend. My experiences fighting for patients and then fighting for myself unleashed this professional, bold spirit that I had only previously known in my personal life.

I also had to embrace me for the unique person that I am.

I am a hood-adjacent California girl who is highly educated, loves Jesus, and loves rap music.

I previously thought that being at "the table" required me to conform to the rules of the table. But I am planning to play by different rules. The table needs a makeover. The front and back tables need people with diverse backgrounds who speak from authentic skin and bring fresh and thought-provoking ideas. As Brené Brown once said, "Don't walk through the world looking for evidence that you don't belong because you will always find it. Don't walk through the world looking for evidence that you're not good enough because you will always find it. Our worth and our belonging are not negotiated with other people."

And now that I am firm on who I am, as Brown put it, "I'm not going to negotiate who I am with [anyone]."

Literally every day, there is a problem that requires bold confidence in its identification and resolution, and I refuse to be the timid one in the corner whispering to the ground.

As such, I adopted the self-proclaimed mantra- "Better every day." Better every day means competing with myself to be a better version of yesterday's me and doing that every single day. Admittingly, I will never be perfect, which is the beauty of this concept; there will always be something to work on.

During medical school, I picked up the phrase "I'll punch you in the face" from a friend's story about a fight that broke out during a road rage incident he witnessed in Nigeria. Throughout my medical training, I held onto that phrase, which oddly provided some support during times of anger and even served as comedic relief on other occasions. However, as I progressed to become a staff physician, I realized that it wasn't appropriate or professional to express myself in such a manner when dealing with others, so I stopped.

Another of the phrases I struggled to stop saying was, "I don't care." I would frequently interrupt people while they were trying to share something important and dismissively say, "I don't care about that." Looking back, I am mortified by my behavior, but it was a common expression that no one called me out on. I began to understand that it was rude and unprofessional, and I have learned better ways to approach those situations. For example, I try to first listen actively and then respond with something like "I have no preference at the moment" or "I don't have a strong opinion either way" if I, in fact, don't have a vested interest in the topic being presented.

These are just a few examples of the many self-corrections I've made in my journey as a leader and in all aspects of my life. I've learned the importance of being mindful of my language and how it can impact others. As a physician, it's crucial to communicate with empathy and professionalism, and I continuously strive to improve and grow in this regard.

I decided to further explore physician leadership which has taken me out of clinical practice full-time. While remaining in the military, this has required leadership training through professional military education and physician leadership training. All while continuing to grow my experience in leadership through my primary work and with our nonprofit organization. There is an endless supply of information in leadership books, podcasts, interactions with other leaders, and everything else I consume that shapes me as a physician leader.

Along the way, I have learned much about myself, who I want to be, and who I want around me when I get there. And once again, I have arrived at a time when new and more difficult decisions must be made - what will I do next?

I don't know about you, but I drew a lot of inspiration from Lin Manuel's interpretation of the life and legacy of Alexander Hamilton. Just as Alexander Hamilton had an insatiable appetite for knowledge and a relentless drive to make a difference, I have embarked on a journey fueled by an inner passion to evolve and create positive change in lives. I am driven by a profound urgency, sensing that time is limited (I'm no Spring chicken) and that each day presents an opportunity to leave my mark on the world, no matter how small. Interestingly, individuals striving for self-improvement often turn to writing, journaling, or expressing themselves in various art forms. These mediums become outlets to explore their thoughts, emotions, and goals, providing a sense of clarity and purpose. This may be the reason behind my writing.

What's next? My writing will continue, my dedication to service will continue, and I will continue to speak out to be heard.

The Next Chapter by Robert Longley
Where you find your courage
Is largely up to you
Many paths and choices
For things that you can do
Choose a path with purpose
You feel within your heart
God will guide you forward
Once your direction starts

There is no one right answer
Do what you feel is right
Pick the path that suits you
And lets you sleep at night

Prepare now for your journey
Your obstacles await
It is you who writes your story
And you who controls your fate

Well, not entirely, Robert, but you were on to something...

# NOTES